Praise for
# THE MAJOR & THE MISSIONARY

"Funny, affectionate, clever, incisive,
moving. Even beyond the many poin
Lewis, Tolkien, and the Inklings, the
their own. They tell a wonderful story

I am sure readers will embrace with great interest and warmth."

—JASON FISHER, former editor of *Mythprint,*
editor of *The Mythopoeic Society*

". . . has the potential to reveal a little-known dimension of Warren
Lewis. His correspondence with a female missionary doctor in
Papua New Guinea is kind, human, broadly-informed, and even
flirtatious. Excerpts read at a recent conference had us alternately on
the edge of our seats, laughing out loud, and on the verge of tears. I
highly recommend it. It's not simply of interest to Lewissians, but
will enchant a far wider audience simply as a record of a charming,
delightful, and ultimately moving epistolary relationship."

—JANET BRENNAN CROFT, author of
*War and the Works of J. R. R. Tolkien* and editor of *Mythlore*

"In addition to the considerable human drama revealed by this
correspondence, it also possesses historical and educational value,
providing insights into a number of social, ecclesiological, mis-
sional, political, and literary issues of the day, both in the United
Kingdom and Papua New Guinea."

—MICHAEL WARD, author of *Planet Narnia*
and *After Humanity: A Guide to C.S. Lewis's* The Abolition of Man

Rabbit Room Press
3321 Stephens Hill Lane
Nashville, TN 37013
info@rabbitroom.com

ISBN 9781951872205
First Edition

Foreword copyright ©2023 John Biggs
Introduction copyright ©2023 Diana Pavlac Glyer
Afterword copyright ©2023 Meredith Goehring
Cover design by Chris Tobias
Photos of Blanche Biggs courtesy of John Biggs

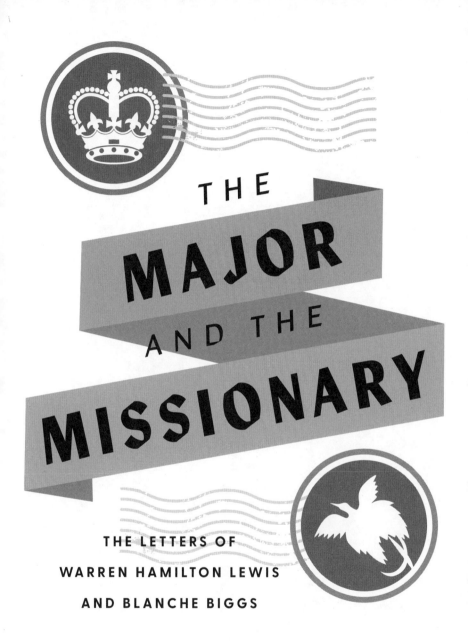

# THE
# MAJOR
## AND THE
# MISSIONARY

### THE LETTERS OF
### WARREN HAMILTON LEWIS
### AND BLANCHE BIGGS

Edited by **DIANA PAVLAC GLYER**

FOREWORD BY JOHN BIGGS · AFTERWORD BY MEREDITH GOEHRING

*Dedicated to generations of Christian missionaries
who left everything behind in order to devote themselves
to loving God and serving others.*

# Contents

# Foreword

These letters between retired army major Warren Lewis and medical missionary Blanche Biggs cover a period of four years, starting from October 1968. Biggs was a missionary working in Papua New Guinea, and Warren, brother to the celebrated Anglican theologian C. S. Lewis, lived in Oxford, England. Warren Lewis had published an edited version of his brother's numerous letters, and Blanche had been reading these letters with much interest as she had been strongly influenced by C. S. Lewis's theological writings.

In her work for the Australian Board of Missions, Blanche had herself written many newsletters to her friends and supporters. She thought they might be of value for posterity, so she initially wrote to Warren to find out how she might go about publishing them. Their correspondence moved from the technicalities of publishing to matters of common interest—thus was their unique relationship born.

Warren was born in Ulster, and although living in England, he was deeply disturbed by The Troubles–the civil war in the

1960s between Ulster and Ireland. After IRA atrocity after atrocity, he developed a deep hatred of the Catholics and a corresponding guilt for harboring that hatred. Indeed, he was convinced that Satan was at work, not only in stirring up The Troubles but also in fostering his abhorrence for the IRA.

Blanche was born in a small country town in far-off Tasmania, a very different background to that of Warren Lewis. She contracted tuberculosis in her youth and had expected to die. She and her mother prayed to God to save her: she lived. She was convinced that God had healed her for a purpose, specifically, to be a medical missionary to do God's work in Papua New Guinea.

Her letters to Warren reveal her stoicism under the sometimes incredible hardships inevitable in a remote mission station in Papua. As a result, she, her colleagues, and her patients were a close-knit family. In her own published newsletters, *From Papua with Love*, she writes of the Papuans, "They taught me many valuable lessons, in loyalty, and in the art of living simply and lovingly."[1]

The common ground between Warren and Blanche was their Anglicanism. Despite quite different backgrounds, their common faith became a springboard for discussing their profound differences, which makes their correspondence so interesting. Warren, a staunch High Churchman, was strongly against ecumenicalism. In the mission field, however, various denominations needed to work together, which

---

1 *From Papua with Love*, a collection of newsletters from the mission field, does not have page numbers. This quotation appears in the preface.

included attending each others' services. Warren was appalled by this, but Blanche embraced it.

Their musical tastes clashed—Blanche was for German classicism, Warren for the French Romantics—but they liked to read the same novels, all with mystical religious overtones, especially those of C. S. Lewis himself. We get a glimpse of the life of the Lewis brothers through a kind of sideways lens.

Their attitudes to sexual behavior were at odds, too. Faced with sexual misconduct among her hospital aides, Blanche took swift action and dismissed the offenders. Warren, on the other hand, thought (as well an ex-army officer might) that boys will be boys. They agreed that these different attitudes were probably due to the respective genders.

These letters contain many examples of how they work through moral dilemmas presented in their very different contexts using their common theological framework.

Here I add a personal note: Blanche was my aunt and godmother. As a child, I saw comparatively little of her, and it was when she retired to live in Brisbane that we grew close. I shared her anger at the greed, hypocrisy, and often sheer cruelty of so many of our "Christian" politicians. I strongly admired her intellectual penetration that cut through what we now call "spin"—honeyed lies meant to deceive.

Some might have perceived Blanche as difficult or prickly, but any such prickliness was dispelled by her evident love for humanity in general, for the underprivileged in particular, and for her own family, of which in later years I was closest to her. Her dealing with people was straightforward, no posturing at all, so that the frank and courageous Blanche who emerges in her letters to Warren Lewis is the same Blanche whom I knew face to face as family.

She died in Brisbane on the 9th May 2008. Her funeral was attended by an astonishing number of friends and admirers. For several years afterward, I received many requests for copies of her book, *From Papua with Love.*

I am so grateful that Diana Pavlac Glyer has edited these letters for this book. They give us a glimpse of the growing relationship between two such different people and how their mutual faith developed that relationship into a special kind of love.

*John Biggs*
Hobart, Tasmania
10 October 2017

# INTRODUCTION
*Diana Pavlac Glyer*

Traveling to the Marion E. Wade Center at Wheaton College is always a pleasure: their collection of materials related to C. S. Lewis, J. R. R. Tolkien, and related authors is so extensive that one is sure to make new discoveries at every visit. In 1998, while doing research for my book about the Inklings, I was astonished to come across a series of letters dated 1968-1978 that contained the complete correspondence between Warren Hamilton Lewis and a missionary doctor named Blanche Biggs.

Why astonished? In part because it is so rare to find *any* collection of letters from the past that exists as a complete set: here, we have all of the letters that passed between them, 87 letters in all, including several quick notes and even some postcards. Typically, scholars who rely on primary texts such as letters are faced with the daunting task of making educated guesses about the larger context. When we have only one side of the conversation, we must take great care as we attempt to reconstruct the tone, content, and questions that constitute the other side. In this collection, we have an unusual opportunity to read every one of the letters that passed between them. Biggs kept carbon copies of her letters, and she carefully saved every single letter she received. Recognizing the value of this rare exchange, she donated all of them to the Wade Center.

But there is another reason that this collection of letters is so remarkable. While a great deal is known about his famous brother, we know comparatively little about Major Warren Hamilton Lewis. This is unfortunate. He is such an interesting person and such an accomplished author; he deserves our best attention.

To complicate matters, some of the information we have about the major can be misleading. Biographies have tended to reduce any discussion of Warren Lewis to a broad-brush summary focused on just two or three traits. The truth is more complex. His personal diary, published under the title *Brothers and Friends*, also presents a challenge. It is not a comprehensive biography; it is not a simple history. For Lewis, his diary fulfilled a particular function. Rather than a neutral record of his thoughts and activities, this diary was a place where Lewis worked out his anger and irritation. Therefore, the tone and attitude we find in those pages is skewed toward criticism and complaints. In the diary, this negativity is not counterbalanced with expressions of the gentle, congenial, happy aspects of his personality. Those who have read the diary have tended to take it at face value, but using the diary as the sole yardstick of Lewis's character gives an inadequate perception of Lewis's nature.

Even more: most of the available material we have, including these diary entries, shows Lewis exclusively in the company of other men or in the confidence of his brother.

This raises numerous questions: How did Warren Lewis address people who were not part of his inner circle? How did he treat new correspondents? How did he interact with women? What do his letters have to say when he is not writing on behalf of C. S. Lewis, answering his brother's fan letters and addressing their questions? And what was life like for Lewis when he lived alone at The Kilns after his famous brother died? The answers to these questions have the power to revise, correct, and extend our understanding of his life and character. The answers to these questions are found in these letters.

## The Major and the Missionary

The first letter in the series comes from Blanche Biggs. She is a missionary doctor and hospital administrator who has been serving in Papua New Guinea for 20 years, 9,000 miles and a world away from Oxford and the home of Major Warren Lewis. Dr. Biggs is a voracious reader and a fan of C. S. Lewis. She has just finished reading *Letters of C. S. Lewis*, a collection lovingly compiled and edited by Warren Lewis following his brother's death.

Biggs is reaching out with a very practical question: "I am writing to find out how these letters survived," she asks (Letter

1).[2] Her interest isn't mere academic curiosity; the question is personal. She has accumulated a significant collection of her own letters and papers, and she is trying to decide whether to save them or to have a bonfire and dispose of them all.

What is striking from this very first letter is Blanche's intelligence and strength. No fawning fangirl, she is observant and articulate. Two qualities that make her an excellent writer. Two qualities she shares with Major Lewis.

How did Lewis respond? With characteristic generosity: "I would strongly urge you neither to burn it or hand it over to anyone else," he says, "but retain it and when you retire, have a go at making a book out of it yourself. I can see from your letter that you are the kind of person who would have no difficulty in writing" (Letter 2). With that encouragement, a friendship is kindled and a correspondence begins.

## PERSONALITY

Those who knew Warren Lewis personally constantly emphasize his warmth and his charity. One of these is Douglas Gresham, C. S. Lewis's stepson. Gresham lived with the Lewis brothers for a time and knew Warren Lewis well. Gresham uses an affectionate nickname as he recalls,

---

2 This and other references identified as "Letter" refer to the letters as they are collected and numbered in this book.

Warnie, a gentleman in all the finest senses of the word, was liked throughout the neighborhood, which, when I arrived, was made up chiefly of the homes of people who worked at the nearby motorcar factories at Cowley. 'The Major' was a well-known and respected figure; always accorded a civil 'Mornin', Major' or 'Arternoon, Major' as he passed by on his regular walks down to Magdalen to work, study or read with Jack in his college rooms during term time.[3]

Joel Heck summarizes, "Warren Lewis was an educated gentleman, a polite man with wit and joviality. He was both a gentle man and a gentleman, impeccable in his manners, talented as a thinker and a writer and a scholar in his own right."[4] His obituary in *The Times* described him as "deeply humble and a warm and delightful companion."[5] And C. S. Lewis once asserted, "he is in so many ways better than I am."[6]

This is not the image most scholars derive from the diaries; it is not the description of Warren Lewis that generally appears in either scholarly or popular accounts of C. S. Lewis's elder brother. As Walter Hooper has observed, careful consideration of this correspondence between Warren Lewis and Blanche Biggs, the major and the missionary, has the power to correct, even rehabilitate, our perception.[7]

---

3 Douglas Gresham, *Lenten Lands* 42.

4 Joel Heck. "Brother's Brother" 8.

5 "Major W. H. Lewis: Soldier and Writer, Obituary." The (London) Times. April 16, 1973.

6 C. S. Lewis. *Collected Letters* I:948-49.

7 Personal conversation with the author, February 17, 2009.

## Issues, Themes, and Topics

As the correspondence unfolds, Warren Lewis and Blanche Biggs share their views on a number of important topics. These themes offer insight into the characters in this drama. They offer practical wisdom as well. Here are some of them:

<u>Spiritual Practice</u>: Warren Lewis spent many years as a wavering atheist/agnostic until  March 4, 1930, when he stood face-to-face with the Great Buddha of Kamakura, a statue in Japan. It was here that he returned to faith in Christ in a moment of mystical significance. He writes,

> I started to say my prayers again after having discontinued doing so for more years than I care to remember: this was no sudden impulse but the result of a conviction of the truth of Christianity which has been growing on me for a considerable time…. I intend to go to Communion once again…. The wheel has now made the full revolution—indifference skepticism, atheism, agnosticism, and back again to Christianity.[8]

Throughout these letters, Lewis writes thoughtfully of his own encounters with God and practice of his faith. Many of the letters exchanged between Biggs and Lewis include discussion of their own religious beliefs and practices, as well as their convictions concerning scripture, worship, and all-too-common tensions among different Christian denominations.

---

8 Qtd. in Hooper, *Companion* 699.

Both see the value of prayer, and both feel inadequate to tackle it. In her work on the mission field, Biggs is well aware that her work depends on God's grace. Nevertheless, she struggles: "Basically of course, spiritual renewal must depend on prayer, and one has so little time and less energy for it" (Letter 10). Lewis sympathizes and elaborates: "One great thing about retirement is that you do have the time for prayer but alas, not always the inclination; but one must stick doggedly to a routine and pray for inclination. My plan is to get up at 6 a.m., make a cup of tea, then pray while the whole world around me is quiet. I've long ago given up the almost universal habit of saying my main prayer last thing at night— about the worst hour one could choose, I think" (Letter 11).

Biggs agrees: "After a lot of painful trial & error, I have come to the same experience as you, that bed-time is the worst possible time for prayer [....] I start my day at 6 with a cup of tea, then prayers, then dress and get ready for the day. So we are alike in that" (Letter 12).

Warren Lewis replies, "Though your 6 a.m. and mine are no doubt at very different times, it gives me much pleasure to think of us both boiling the kettle and settling down to prayers at our own six a.m.s" (Letter 13).

Where does one find help for a tepid prayer life? Both turn to the Anglican *Book of Common Prayer*. Warren Lewis began each day with the morning collects, then the Lord's prayer, then adds what he calls his own "blundering extempore efforts." He concludes, "but however approached, prayer is never easy, is it?" (Letter 57).

<u>The Nature of Scripture</u>: Lewis also made Bible reading a regular part of his practice, and he held a high view of scripture. When challenged with new translations, he said, "I was born conservative and hate all change, but obviously we cannot cling to the old [King James] Bible for the beauty of its diction. It isn't a literary treat to be savored in an idle moment, but a guidebook to a rule of life" (Letter 41).

Despite his reliance on the Bible as a guidebook, he frankly admits that he finds some parts of it challenging, particularly the epistles of St. Paul: "Of the Epistles, my brother used to say that he wished that God, in entrusting Paul with His message, had also seen fit to give him the capacity of orderly arrangement of his ideas. Even James found Paul hard to understand, you may remember" (Letter 41).

<u>Church Attendance</u>: Lewis attended Holy Trinity Church, a short and easy walk from his home. Like his brother, he disliked most church music and preferred the 8 a.m. communion service. Not only did this early service have the advantage of being "said" rather than sung, it also attracted fewer congregants. As Lewis admits, "I'm rather ashamed to confess that I get more good from a sparsely attended service 'when two or three are gathered together.' But I'm quite wrong of course, one ought to wish for a crowded church" (Letter 23).

<u>The Concept of Mere Christianity</u>: And what of his brother's emphasis on mere Christianity? Lewis remained skeptical of it. This single issue provides one of the most persistent points of contention between Lewis and Biggs; their contrasting

views of church union is a theme in these letters from beginning to end. Biggs not only embraced ecumenism on the mission field, she even sponsored conferences and other events
to encourage dialogue and collaboration among different
denominations. Like Lewis, she was Anglican, but happily
worshiped with Roman Catholic friars and worked alongside
Lutherans, Congregationalists, Presbyterians, and others.

On the other hand, Warren Lewis staunchly resisted
combined churches: "I'm all in favour of the closest collaboration between the various churches in that large field of
work which they have in common; but no 'watering down of
belief.' And union without such a watering down seems to me
to be an impossibility" (Letter 6).

In support of this view, he cites a debate that was affecting
him at home: The "chief bone of contention here is the proposed amalgamation of the Church of England with the
Methodists—to which I'm violently opposed. It can only be
done by compromise, which makes nonsense of doctrine. If
we are right, why do the Methodists not come over to us? Or,
if they are right, why don't we join them?" (Letter 4).

For Lewis, the issue wasn't just about doctrine; it concerned
practice. Communion was a particular concern: "To take the
most important of all points—Communion administered
by anyone other than an ordained priest of my own Church
would not be a Sacrament at all, but a mere ritual commemorating the Last Supper. Of the Seventh Day Adventists I
know nothing except the name; but how the Salvation Army,
which I understand does not believe in <u>any</u> Sacraments, can
unite with us is more than I can understand. In fact I don't

get as far as understanding what such a Communion means"
(Letter 6).

Biggs addresses the matter head-on—winsome, personal,
and yet unwavering: "I agree with you that the essential beliefs
of our Church must not be watered down; but I think that
much of our difference lies in emphasis rather than contradiction. I would be quite ready to receive Communion according
to another rite, and even if it were a commemoration conducted by a man not ordained according to our ideas, I would
not feel a hypocrite if I partook, believing that it was no more
than a commemoration, and not giving it a value that it did
not deserve. Maybe that would be an example of 'going the
second mile'?" (Letter 7).

Biggs invites Lewis again and again to reconsider this
issue. In the end, Lewis does come around to her point of
view, but it is not her persistence, her careful arguments, or
her loving example that changes him. Late in their correspondence, in September of 1970, Warren Lewis has an experience
that wins him over at last. That story is told in these pages.
As he relates the tale to Biggs, she does not respond with
arrogance or a smug "I told you so," but rather with wisdom
and utmost kindness: "I absolutely agree that the cure of our
prejudices is to get to know people and find out that they are
not fire-eating dragons" (Letter 37).

The Troubles: Lewis's personal suspicion of the ecumenical
movement is played out against a larger and much more
violent backdrop. In 1968, the tension in Northern Ireland
erupted into riots, bombings, and protests. More than 3,500

people were killed during the period known as the Troubles, and more than half of those killed were civilians. Many of the worst events of that period happened in the years covered by these letters and are mentioned here: the Battle of the Bogside, the Springhill Massacre, and the shooting death of 17-month-old Angela Gallagher.

Born and raised in Ulster, Warren Lewis was deeply shaken by these events:

> my poor Ulster is passing through a bad patch, but I've seen many such before. The tragedy is that Protestant and Catholic are, one can say, <u>born</u> hating each other. I'm 3rd generation Ulster on my father's side and on my mother's, 5th" (Letter 11). Lewis had been dealing first hand with the tension between Protestant and Catholic since childhood. When he was a boy, his mother had hired a cook and a housemaid who were Roman Catholics. This angered some of the neighbors, local Protestants who expressed their rage by writing disparaging messages in chalk on the walls of their home. Notes were put through the mail slot, too, including one that said, "Send the dirty papists back to the Devil where they belong".[9]

The conflict deepened. Lewis writes, "Poor Ulster, things are if anything rather worse than better, and the last outrage has worried even the English—15 lbs of gelignite as a booby trap on the unlocked door of an abandoned car, which blew two policemen into small fragments—the cold blooded

---

9 George Sayer, 35.

wickedness of it! It might have just as easily been a bunch of school children who decided to investigate that car" (Letter 34). The issue continues on the world stage, and it remains a topic that stirs anger, frustration, grief, and pain throughout these letters.

History: In addition to the upheaval in Ulster, there were other notable historical events mentioned in these pages. Biggs and Lewis offer contemporary comments on other tense situations, including the attempted murder of Pope Paul VI, Senator Edward "Ted" Kennedy and the Chappaquiddick incident, Malcolm Muggeridge's controversial television appearances, the abdication of the Duke of Windsor from the throne, and race riots occasioned by the South African Springboks rugby team. Happier historical events are mentioned, too. For example, both are astonished by the Apollo 11 lunar landing, although both express concern about the exorbitant price tag of space exploration.

One historic thread that connects us with both Biggs and Lewis is unflagging interest in the activities of Queen Elizabeth II. Interest in the British monarchy hasn't changed, and several letters refer to the Queen. In 1970, she toured much of Australia, accompanied by Prince Philip, Princess Anne, and Charles, then Prince of Wales.

In March of 1972, Biggs reads in the newspaper that J. R. R. Tolkien has gone to Buckingham Palace to be presented with a CBE, or Commander of the Most Excellent Order of the British Empire, from the Queen. This rank is one below knighthood, awarded for leadership or service rendered regionally or nationally. Three years later, on 1 January 1975, Biggs herself received an honor from the Queen: an OBE, or Officer of the Most Excellent Order of the British Empire. An OBE is granted to those who have performed admirable service in the arts, sciences, public services, or philanthropy.

There are other important current events, more personal and direct. Biggs describes her work after the Mount Lamington volcano erupted: It killed 4,000 people, and her hospital made room for more than 1,000 additional patients who were sick, injured, or displaced by the blast. The mission hospital adapted to floods, winds, and limited resources: power outages, inconsistent telephone service, limited supplies, and insufficient staff. As a missionary doctor, Biggs performed surgeries and delivered babies, but most of her work was oriented toward dealing with patients suffering from either tuberculosis (TB) or leprosy. Biggs attended many professional conferences. At one of them, she enjoyed the opportunity to hear a lecture from renowned anthropologist Margaret Mead.

And in Oxford, Lewis faced food shortages and endless strikes: car ferry crews, mail strike, coal strike, railway strike, and a dock strike, too. The worst of them all was the rubbish disposal strike in October of 1970, a situation so serious it made headlines worldwide. Lewis writes, "Every day, millions of gallons of polluted water is being rationed and of course all the streets are piled high with what would normally be the contents of our ash bins" (Letter 38). Biggs is very concerned about the health implications of the sewage workers remaining on strike long term. But Lewis is more concerned about the workers: "for once, my sympathy is with the strikers, whose wage is pretty near the hardship line. Where or when—if ever—the wage spiral is going to be checked, we none of us know" (Letter 38).

Lewis, Tolkien, and Books: My discovery of these letters began as I searched for first-hand accounts of the Inklings. These letters do not disappoint. Blanche Biggs peppers Lewis with questions about these authors: Who is among them? Do they still gather? Where? When? These letters provide one of the few first-hand accounts of the Inklings in the period just after C. S. Lewis's death.

During this time, Biggs is reading Hadfield's *Introduction to Charles Williams* along with one of Williams' novels. She writes, "It is a pity that such reading is of necessity superficial; I am too tired to do more than skim over his thoughts and ideas. He must have been a wonderful friend. It is excellent, but it is not food for a tired brain" (Letter 28).

Lewis replies: "Yes, Charles Williams <u>was</u> a wonderful friend and one of the very best men I've ever met in addition to being a very brilliant one. Oddly enough I'm re-reading one of his novels myself at the moment with that care which the job demands; for no one could describe Charles as an easy author. Did I ever tell you how his friendship with my brother began? Each wrote the other a fan letter and the two crossed in the post!"

Biggs struggled to read Charles Williams, but she was unabashed in her enthusiasm for Joy Davidman: "We are trying to help us all spiritually and to grow in Christian love by having weekly Bible Study classes. They are not my line of country at all, but anyway we are all trying. After a rather unfruitful study of St. James' epistle we have now come on to Joy Davidman's *Smoke on the Mountain*, a book that I have read and admired several times. We seem able to build more on her than on St. James!" (Letter 10).

Lewis and Biggs are wonderful writers; both are avid readers. Books mentioned here include a wide range of authors, genres, moods, and topics: Shakespeare's *Midsummer Night's Dream*, J. B. Phillips' *Ring of Truth*, Woodforde's *Diary of a Country Parson*, Donald Caskie's *Tartan Pimpernel*, Edith Bone's *Seven Years Solitary*, and Dietrich Bonhoeffer's *Letters and Papers from Prison*. Many titles by C. S. Lewis are discussed as well: *Reflections on the Psalms, The Four Loves, Miracles, Christian Reflections,* The Chronicles of Narnia, and *The Screwtape Letters*, among others.

Biggs also asks Lewis about his own books, and he replies, "I fancy that all my books are out of print; at least they have long ago ceased <u>paying</u> anything. You wouldn't care for them unless you are interested in 17th-century France (the only subject I know anything about). I've got a spare copy of one of them, and if you think you would really read it I'll get it off to you as a Christmas present!" (Letter 13). He sends her a copy of *The Sunset of the Splendid Century*, saying, "I'm pleased to hear that you at any rate propose to read my book and am only sorry that it isn't a better one. I like it least of any of mine" (Letter 23).

Least favorite or not, Biggs is pleased to receive it: "Knowing that you and your brother wrote such imaginative things as boys, I wonder that I ever expected your writing to be statistical and unimaginative. You must have had a lot of fun reading up all these old records, letters, etc., and then breathing your own kind of life into them." She concludes, "It makes excellent reading" (Letter 22).

C. S. Lewis's Legacy: After C. S. Lewis died, Warren Lewis continued to live at The Kilns. He spent time with friends, edited his brother's letters, and did more writing. What did it look like for Warren Lewis to live on as the steward of his brother's legacy?

Fan letters kept coming, and Lewis spent hours answering them. He writes, "I continue the steady two hours a day six days a week labour of answering his letters" (Letter 72). Neither Warren Lewis nor C. S. Lewis liked the mail, but both felt an obligation to answer by return post. Biggs is amazed by this commitment, "that your brother could drive himself on to write letters when it was a job he did not like, and when he was in pain and "cab-horse tired" (I think that is a wonderfully descriptive expression). To compare it with my own smaller efforts, I know the fatigue, but I like writing letters as well as receiving them—do you?" (Letters 60). He didn't.

But letters kept coming, and more: The Kilns was besieged with tourists: "Ungracious though it may sound, I'm suffering from a spate of visitors, nearly all American, who gate-crash here to say they have been inside the house where "the gre-ate C. S. Loois" wrote. They seem to regard me as the custodian of a national monument, open to visitors daily 10am to 6pm!" Though the complaint is sharp, here (as with other angry outbursts), it is rapidly resolved with gratitude: "But Lord bless them, it is something to know that interest in my brother is still so common [...] so really, I have little excuse for grumbling" (Letter 9).

There was one visitor Lewis welcomed gladly. Wheaton College professor Clyde S. Kilby made regular trips to England, often bringing a small group of students with him. Lewis refers to him as "a dear American friend" and clearly enjoys the chance to visit local tourist sites together (Letter 48).

Life on the Mission Field: I discovered these letters because my scholarly focus is on Lewis, Tolkien, and the Inklings. In digging through the letters of Warren Lewis, I was on the hunt for insights into the inner workings of that writing group, first-hand accounts of what they said to each other and what difference it made to the books they were writing.

My first delight in finding this particular set of letters was to read all the comments about Tolkien, Williams, and the meetings of the Inklings that continued even after C. S. Lewis had died. But the more I spent time studying these letters, the more interested I became in Dr. Blanche Biggs. She was a remarkable woman of significant accomplishments.

In presenting this book and in writing the stage play that serves as a companion to it, what has motivated me more than anything else is the responsibility of telling her story. She came to represent generations of missionaries who left the comforts of home and family to obey Christ and serve others.

The locations and details vary, but the heart of it is the same: Those who have devoted their lives to missionary service do not expect to be heralded, but they do deserve to be known. When we seek to understand Blanche Biggs, to hear her voice firsthand, and to honor the letters that she believed were good for little more than fueling a bonfire, we help to give a name and a face to the tens of thousands who have lived in foreign nations, giving their lives in sacrifice and service.

## A Story Worth Telling

I have been astonished by the completeness of this series of letters, by the insight they offer into the life and personality of Warren Lewis, by their account of the Inklings, by the rich glimpse of history that they provide, and by their vivid portrayal of day-to-day life on the mission field. There is one other aspect worth noting: these letters offer a compelling story, a strong narrative of a relationship that progresses year by year.

This correspondence begins in the simplest way: Blanche Biggs is writing a letter to an author she admires, thanking him and asking for advice. She is thinking she might write a book someday. Should she continue to collect materials, pass the project on to someone else, write it herself, or let it go? Lewis is generous and encouraging in his response. Perhaps he is pleased that someone has written to him about his books. Perhaps he is drawn to her insight and obvious skill as a writer. It is possible he is reminded of the way that Joy Davidman once sent a letter to C. S. Lewis and the unexpected way that their love story unfolded.

No matter the reasons, Warren and Blanche become pen pals, or, as they would have put it, pen friends. The early letters of the late 1960s explore their world travels, the particularities of publishing, their work on church committees, world events, vacations, weather, and, of course, books. They describe various ailments and illnesses, as one might expect of friends in middle age. Biggs sends Lewis a copy of a magazine produced by the Anglican Mission. Lewis responds, "What a pleasant surprise it was to open your magazine and there to meet you, if not in the flesh at any rate by camera" (Letter 11). A year into the correspondence, Biggs notes, "This correspondence has come a long way from the discussion of writing books which began it" and "I am developing a mental picture of you, incomplete in some respects, but each letter fills in a bit more" (Letter 10; Letter 16).

But in February of 1970, the connection deepens. "January has been a terrible month, maybe the hardest month I have had in the service" (Letter 18). Biggs is faced with a scandal at the hospital, and she is overwhelmed by the implications. She reaches out to Lewis for comfort and advice, and he does not respond well. She berates him and then expresses regret: "I still don't know if it was right or wrong of me to pour out my troubles in your last letter. There are so many people one cannot pour them out to, and you and my sister [Win] seemed to be a sympathetic and uninvolved ear to besiege" (Letter 20).

Biggs makes her way through the tricky situation, and the two of them argue their way through the aftermath. The result is deeper trust and a new level of increasingly personal sharing. Lewis concludes, "be assured that if you care to unburden yourself to me, you will find a sympathetic even if unhelpful listener" (Letter 21).

A year later, in Spring 1971, another shift occurs. Biggs has been signing her letters "with all good wishes" or "yours very sincerely." Now she closes with "yours, affectionately" (Letter 45). "My dear Major Lewis," she writes. "You have been much in my thoughts" (Letter 46). They exchange photographs. Biggs puts the picture of Lewis in her prayer book, using it as a bookmark for her daily office, and, therefore, is "often reminded of you" (Letter 56). Biggs invites Lewis to use first names, and in a short, handwritten note, Lewis replies: "I'm flattered at the invitation to use your Xtian name on the understanding that you will reciprocate with 'Dear Warren'" (Letter 61). Biggs responds, "I feel much more comfortable now that we are Warren and Blanche!" (Letter 62). Now both sign their letters "with affection."

Later that same year, in September 1971, Biggs discusses the schedule for an upcoming furlough, which tentatively includes a plan to visit England. Lewis responds directly and with candor: "Many thanks for your interesting letter of the 5th. The most interesting thing you have to tell me is that you may be in this country around May 1973, and if I am still alive then we must make plans for a meeting; wouldn't it be fun? So I shall live in hopes" (Letter 55). Hope is kindled, and hope is deferred. The letters tell the story.

## An Invitation

Insights into Warren Lewis, C. S. Lewis, and the Inklings. A snapshot of life on the mission field during the burgeoning ecumenical movement. Thoughts on matters of faith and the tragic, heart-warming, and comical events of the recent past. Topics such as great books, spiritual practice, and the ever-present challenge of balancing competing obligations. A compelling, unfolding personal story.

The larger context of these letters, carefully preserved, raises more capacious questions: What are *we* to do with the letters and papers we accumulate over a lifetime? What is the role of archives and study centers, like the Marion E. Wade Center? How should we incline ourselves to the witness of history? And what is our responsibility in remembering those who have gone before us and in being faithful to tell their stories?

In bringing these wonderful letters to print, I invite you to take a seat at the table, to enter into the process of research. Examine these primary documents, imagine their setting, and taste the experience of history, of a time and place quite different from our own.

And more: follow along in a compelling drama, as two strangers—wise, articulate, passionate, mature followers of Christ—become pen pals, then friends and confidants. Listen to their voices. Watch hope rise as they make plans to finally meet face to face. Their story is rich in insight. It is deeply human and profoundly moving. Hearing their own story in their own words has changed my life. I hope it will touch yours.

*Editorial Note*: These letters have been lightly edited in order to avoid unnecessary distractions. Some typing errors have been corrected. Some missing words (generally due to failure of the carbon paper) have been supplied. Some formatting changes have been made. Where typos, gaps, abbreviations, punctuation, regionalisms, and so forth do not interfere with clarity, they have been left to stand as is.

*The letters begin in October 1968,
almost 5 years after C. S. Lewis's death.*

5 October 1968

Dear Major Lewis,

I hope that you have the patience in answering letters from strangers that your brother had. This letter is written from curiosity, but there is some sort of purpose behind it.

I am just finishing the *C. S. Lewis Letters* edited by you, and of course I bought it only because so many others of his books have been a help and enjoyment to me in the past. Your book rounds out one's mental picture of your brother in a most satisfying way.

Now to the question: how did all those letters survive, so as to be available to you for publication? You say that you acted as his secretary for years, and that suggests typewritten letters with a carbon copy retained; but some of the letters seem to have been written hastily by Professor Lewis himself and probably by hand. Not many people store up old letters in this day and age, though I can remember seeing many old letters of my Father's, and a few of my Mother's kept for many years; I suppose that the family burned them at the time of their death. Not many children would keep the originals of letters received by their parents and relations. If you did obtain letters from the recipients, it must have required a tremendous amount of work on your part, and a large number of people storing up old letters to have them available. It is especially hard to understand how the letters written by your brother to his and your father can have survived; surely a young man would not keep carbons; and if, as seems likely, C. S. Lewis had the task of clearing out your father's possessions after his death, it does not seem likely that he would retain his own old letters.

My curiosity is prompted by a similar situation. I am a born hoarder of letters and records, always with the feeling that they may be needed some day. Any letters of importance I always type and keep a carbon (especially as much of my correspondence is official or semi-official) and now I have a 20-year collection stowed away and always have the intention at the back of my mind to have a sorting and burning campaign, and of course never find the time.

Some of my letters and papers might be useful in the future, even after my death, not because of their merit in themselves; but I have been a missionary doctor living in this same area for 20 years, and I have seen this Territory developing right under my nose, from primitive life to a pseudo-civilized one.[10] Also our own Diocese and its work

---

10 The territory referred to here is Papua New Guinea, which occupies the eastern half of the island of New Guinea off the north-east corner of Australia. Biggs arrived there on September 7, 1948, and served as the first Medical Co-ordinator for the Anglican Church of Papua New

has grown in size and scope over the same period.[11] I have a hope that after his death, our former Bishop's diary may be published.[12] He once said to us that his war-time diaries could not be published in his lifetime; he was in the thick of the Papuan campaign both among Headquarters Army staff, and helping the most ignorant labourer among the natives conscripted to help. (No, I don't think they were conscripted).

It is just a question whether, when the time comes for me to resign, I just have a grand bonfire, or hand over all this correspondence to the Mission authorities to use if they wish. I doubt if I have the ability at my age to write anything myself (I am nearing 60) when I do find myself with some leisure—if ever!

Incidentally, I had read Joy Davidman's book *Smoke on the Mountain* a long time before I knew that she was more than an acquaintance of your brother. His Foreword of course

---

Guinea. She was part of a group of "Diocesan Medical Evangelists" who served under the auspices of the Australian Board of Missions. Their ministry was defined as a specific call "to go further in special training and service in the field of medical research and medicare— using the compassion, the meteria medica, and the skills which the good God provides for His sick and separated family" (Hand).

11 The Anglican Church is divided into districts, called "dioceses," each one under the care of a bishop.

12 Sir Philip Nigel Warrington Strong (1899-1983) was the Bishop of New Guinea from 1937 until 1963 and Primate of Australia from 1966 to 1970. The wartime diaries mentioned here refer to Strong's daily journal, a portion of which he permitted to be edited by David Wetherell and published in 1981 as *The New Guinea Diaries of Philip Strong 1936-45*.

announced that much. I was very much impressed by it.[13]

Thank you for the labour and skill you have put into the [*the letter ends here*].

---

13 Joy Davidman and C. S. Lewis met in 1952 and were married in 1956. They influenced each other's written work before and during their marriage. *Smoke on the Mountain* is a unique interpretation of the Ten Commandments, with a foreword written by C. S. Lewis.

## 2

22 October 1968

Dear Dr. Biggs,

I must apologize for the delay in replying to your kind and interesting letter of the 5th, but it was only 48 hours ago that I got back from a fortnight's holiday—and I make it a rule when I go away never to have any letters forwarded.[14]

Now to the survival of the letters. My father died in 1929 and as I was a serving army officer and my brother established in Oxford, there seemed to be no use in maintaining the old home, which was broken up and sold. Our father was an inveterate hoarder, and when we came to examine his papers we found that he had never destroyed <u>anything</u>—not even the stubs of his used cheque books. All this material was shipped over to my brother's rooms in Magdalen College, Oxford,

---

14 Warren Lewis had been on vacation October 6-20 with two close friends, Len (Leonard) and Mollie (Maud) Miller. They stayed in Westons, Walberswick, in Suffolk at the home of June Freud, and they spent their days walking to the beach, shopping, reading, and watching television. Warren went on vacation with the Millers regularly, once or twice each year.

and we decided vaguely to sort it out at some future date.[15] I retired in 1931 and came to live in Oxford myself. I had not begun to write in those days and wanted some occupation, so I went through this mass of documents, and decided—more or less as a joke—that I should compile and type "The Lewis Papers." This I did, including diaries in addition to letters, and covering a period 1850-1930. When I completed the job in 1935 all the material with the exception of certain diaries, was burnt by my brother. I still have my typescript which ran to eleven 4vo. volumes.[16]

As regards your own material I would strongly urge you neither to burn it or hand it over to anyone else, but retain it and when you retire, have a go at making a book out of it yourself. I can see from your letter that you are the kind of person who would have no difficulty in writing and I regard "nearing 60" as middle age—being myself 73. I had no experience in writing—except official minutes—when I got my first book published at 58; and my seventh and last was written when I was 69.[17] Another reason why I think you should have a shot at it is that very little has been published about the vast area which you live in. The Caribbean, Latin America, and China have all been done to death, but I do not remember

---

15 C. S. Lewis had been a don at Magdalen College, Oxford, since 1925.

16 "4vo." refers to the size of the loose sheets of paper that made up the typescript, also known as a "quarto." The bound volumes of the Lewis Family Papers measure 10.25" x 7.75" and are housed at the Marion E. Wade Center in Wheaton, Illinois.

17 Warren Lewis's first published book is *The Splendid Century*. All seven of his histories deal with 17th and 18th century France.

anything worth reading about Oceania since [Robert Louis] Stevenson's time; and anyway so far as I remember he never worked down as far south as Papua.

I wonder if your Philip Strong was any relation of the "Tommy" Strong who was Bishop of Oxford when I first came to live here?[18] Possibly my brother may have known the man you mention, but I do not remember ever having heard him refer to him.

It gives me real pleasure to learn that you enjoyed my brother's *Letters*, though regret that they should have shortened your nights. But I fancy Papuan nights—you appear to be on the Line [i.e., the equator]—are short in any case; I know from experience that Singapore ones are anyway![19]

with kind wishes, yours sincerely, W. H. Lewis

---

18 Sir Thomas Banks Strong GBE, DD (1861–1944). Thomas Strong was Bishop of Ripon from 1920 to 1925, when he became Bishop of Oxford. He served in Oxford until 1937. Strong became a Knight Grand Cross of the Order of the British Empire in 1918.

19 Warren went to Hong Kong in May of 1927, stopping in Singapore along the way. For more details about his time overseas, see Joel D. Heck's "Chronologically Lewis" at http://www.joelheck.com/.

3

7 December 1968

Dear Major Lewis,

I have been a long time writing to thank you for your kind letter of October 22nd. I have carried your letter around the Territory as I have gone here and there in connection with my work, on the assumption that one has more time for writing when one is away; but of course it is a fallacy. I even had four days in the Highlands, at over 5000 feet (4-blanket-and-hot-water-bag-place) where one's energy increases very greatly; but even that was not a success. Here on the plains we are in the middle of the "wet season," where humidity slows up activity quite a lot.[20]

Thank you for your suggestion that I keep my own old letters and use them for writing a book myself. A friend of mine in Australia has been saying the same thing to me

---

20 In the highlands, the weather would be more mild during the day and cool in the evening. In Popondetta, however, the heat and humidity kept temperatures very warm. During December, the weather would be determined by the North-West Monsoon airstream.

for some time. I have little confidence in my ability to do it <u>well</u>; the interest of the material would have to carry the book through the publisher's hands, rather than my ability to use it well.[21] My future is still much veiled. I meant to retire at 60, partly to be young enough to make myself a new life under such different circumstances, and partly because I have seen old members of staff stay on too long in the service, thinking they were "helping" and in reality being quite a burden on their colleagues. I told the Bishop as much, and he made it clear that he needed the experience of the "old hands" and that perhaps a lighter job might be found in due course. For this year I have been doing a job of my colleague on long leave in England as well as my own, and have got through it by the grace of God. As soon as he returns (he is at present at the Mayo Clinic) I shall go off on my leave.

I wonder if you would give me some advice in case I do at some time adopt your suggestion of writing a book? <u>You</u> should know all the answers! For instance, if you publish a letter received from, or written to, someone else, is it necessary to get their written permission to use it? Or would one do it only in the event of possible copyright complications, or out of courtesy if publication might cause embarrassment? Or does one get over it by merely informing them that one is planning a book and may use material provided by them? In the case of the writer of such material having died, would it be necessary to get permission from his executors or family?

---

21 The friend mentioned here is probably Sister Jean Henderson, who worked with Biggs at St. Luke's Hospital in Eroro.

I gather from a friend of mine who had published a lot of articles (no books) that the choice of a publisher is very important, each publishing firm having its own special interest and scope. I should think the sensible thing would be to examine other books on this country and see where they were published. Actually, there has been a lot written, from serious anthropological writers down to the casual visitor who stays here for a few weeks and then writes as an authority. In spite of your suggestion, I would have thought the market might well be glutted!

Our Bishop Philip Strong (now Primate of Australia) is not related to the former Bishop of Oxford.[22] His brother is a doctor now practising in Windsor, but his Oxford home will have been broken up.

A letter received yesterday from a teacher who spent a holiday with us said "Remembering your interest in C. S. Lewis, I am sending you one of his books for Christmas." Now I am wondering which one; also when I shall find time to read it!

I think your brother's chief gift to bewildered Christians was to clear away starry-eyed sentiment [*words cut off at bottom of page*]

I admire <u>your</u> courage in launching out into authorship at a fairly late age and successfully producing seven of them. Why stop at the age of 73? It is a pity that I have not come across any; our contact with books is rather haphazard, of course.

---

22 A primate is the senior bishop or archbishop who is responsible to oversee one of the approximately 40 provinces that comprise the worldwide Anglican Communion.

Wishing you a happy Christmas, (and not as strenuous as ours!)

Yours sincerely,[23]

---

23 We do not have the original letters from Biggs, only the carbon copies that she saved and then donated to The Marion E. Wade Center. These copies are not signed.

17 December 1968

Dear Miss Biggs,

Thanks for your interesting letter of the 7th and for your Christmas good wishes—which I'm afraid I shall be too late to reciprocate, so instead I wish you a very happy 1969.

Sorry to hear that (for unexplained reasons) your hill station holiday was not a success, for I should have thought an escape from tropical to hot water bottle conditions would have been heaven. I've never served anywhere where there <u>was</u> a hill station, but I've all the experience I want of damp heat all the year round.

Yes, I know well what you mean about hanging on too long. When I was younger I did a good deal of church work up to Diocesan level, and can recall what a hindrance to business the dear old "has beens" were, and the impossibility of hurting them deeply by suggesting that the time had come for them to retire.[24] I don't know how closely you are in touch

---

24  Lewis served on the vestry at Holy Trinity Church (Headington Quarry) as a church warden from about 1952 until 1957.

with Church affairs here at the moment, but the chief bone
of contention is the proposed amalgamation of the Church
of England with the Methodists—to which I'm violently
opposed.[25] It can only be done by compromise which makes
nonsense of doctrine. If we are right, why do the Methodists
not come over to us, or vice versa, why don't we join them?

As regards book material, I don't know if any legal obligation exists to obtain permission for the reproduction of a
letter written to you, but obviously it would be a matter of
courtesy to do so. The point did not much arise in my own
case, as I was collecting material written by my brother, not
to him. I circularized every likely person for the loan of his
letters, and took this as implying permission.

As regards choice of a publisher, you will find touting
your own wares a heartbreaking business. Much the best
thing to do is to send the MS to a literary agent and let him
do the donkey work; he will know far better than you ever
can, which House would be likely to publish your book, and
you will find it well worth the 10% you have to pay for his
services. Whether you would be entering a glutted market, I
don't know, but I doubt it. I'm a fairly constant reader of travel
and similar books, and cannot recollect having come across
anything about Papua. My agent has always done me very
well and is a nice man, and when things are a bit "forrader"

---

25 The Methodist Church proposed reunification with the Church
of England in the 1960s. This caused controversy between the two
churches, which continued until the General Synod of 1972 when the
proposition was denied by the Church of England's governing body.

I'll send you his address with Pleasure.[26]

What you say about answers to Prayer is true—but cannot most of us when looking back over our lives, remember prayers which we are now very thankful were <u>not</u> granted?

Winter has now set in after a summer which lasted for 48 hours. You may wish yourself over here, but if I had a magic carpet I'd be on a tropic beach where you have to wear shoes to the water's edge on account of the heat of the sand!

with all best wishes, yours sincerely, W. H. Lewis

---

26 Lewis used Curtis Brown as agent for many of his books. That may be the agent he is referencing here.

# 5

30 March 1969

My dear Major Lewis

I should have written long before this to thank you for the helpful advice sent in your letter of 17<sup>th</sup> December. I had a very busy January, and came home (i.e. to my sister's home [in Tasmania]) on leave at the beginning of February; and was too weary in mind and spirit to do more than essential jobs.[27] It was also a joy to have the luxuries (by comparison) of civilized life, with furlough money to spend and interesting things to spend it on, theatres, films, books etc. I must soon go back to the Mission, and no one can deny that the life is absorbing, but it is very demanding. There is already a sense of "girding up the loins" for the coming effort.

If and when I retire and attempt writing (about which I still have strong doubts) I shall be very glad to accept any help you can give me in the matter. I would not have thought of employing an agent had you not recommended it. Much

---

27 Biggs' sister Winifred (known as Win) had a home in Hobart. Biggs stayed with her periodically.

easier, and it would ease the sorrow if one's effort did not find favour with any publisher at all!

I am surprised that you have not come across any literature on Papua New Guinea. Just on this leave without any special hunting I have acquired or read 3 books about P. N. G. in the war; one called *Prisoner's Base and Home Again* by our own beloved James Benson, a priest taken prisoner by the Japs and for a long time kept with Roman Catholic missionaries in a camp in New Britain;[28] also I have a book written at the turn of the century by one of our missionaries; and a recent one on the country by J. K. McCarthy, who only recently retired after being Director of Native Affairs for years.[29] Also a not-very-good one by Michael Courage, son of the Courage of beer fame, who worked with our Mission as a V. S. O.[30] There are stacks more on the market!

It is interesting to know that you once worked in some Diocesan office or similar set-up; I do in a sense, as I am at present a member of the Standing Committee, which runs the Diocese in between Conferences. We are now working out a Constitution and becoming a sister Diocese of the Australian ones, instead of a missionary one. The next Conference in June

---

28 New Britain is the largest island in the Bismark Archipelago of Papua New Guinea.

29 James Benson was an English priest and artist who joined the staff in 1920. He was taken prisoner by the Japanese in 1942 and released in 1945.

30 "V. S. O." stands for Volunteer Service Organization; Michael Courage was a volunteer sent from England. Courage Brewery was founded in London in 1787.

will appoint a true Synod, but it remains to be seen if I will still take an active part, as this Conference will be by election.[31] It is interesting to be on the Committee at this formative stage. We have the previous Administrator of P. N. G., Sir Donald Cleland, as the Chancellor of our Diocese and he is in effect drawing up the new Constitution.

Maybe the younger Churches out here are more ready for unity, if not for union, than the longer-established Churches in the Mother country. I find even that New Guinea Churches are more closely and less self-consciously getting together than the Churches in Australia. It is not of course a matter of watering down belief, but of consulting together, working together and even of making friendships on a personal basis. All this is possibly more important and less controversial than a unity based on common beliefs in the detailed sense. We have a Melanesian Council of Churches, and it demands agreement with a skeleton of dogma; the Salvation Army had to take deep thought before they agreed to join, though they strongly wished to. As far as I know, the Seventh Day Adventists, who are very strong in New Guinea, have not joined. On the basis of co-operation I believe that the more we have, the better; though it is bound to bring out differences all the more strongly, on which some adaptation will have to be worked out. After all, there is a wide gap between the High and Low branches of the C. of E. both in dogma and in practice, yet we rub along pretty happily under the C. of E. label.[32] I must admit that I would be spiritually starved

31 A synod is a council or assembly of clergy members within the church.

32 The Church of England has been described as having three different

if I had to worship a la Methodism always; yet one can be spiritually starved in the C. of E., even in Papua where the singing is unaccompanied, and frightful to listen to; and the sermon probably on a kindergarten level, translated into one or even two other languages! One has to accept it for the sake of the "weaker brethren."

I am sorry you had such a poor summer; maybe the coming one will be kinder. My sister and I were so lucky in 1964, when the Summer went on and on.[33] We both dream of another trip, though possibly not together, as our times to resign from our jobs may well be different.

With all good wishes, yours sincerely,

---

approaches, referred to as the high church (Anglo-Catholic), the low church (Evangelical), and the broad church (Liberal). They differ in doctrine, traditions, and liturgical structure.

33  Biggs and her sister Win left Papua on long leave in 1964. They spent most of their time in Britain but also made a number of other short trips, including a visit to the Holy Land.

6

Easter Day
6 April 1969

Dear Miss Biggs,

Whilst it is useless to wish you a happy and profitable Easter, I can hope it for you as I type—and to hear in due course how and where you spent it.

Though I don't know anything except what you have told me of your Mission field, oddly enough I've just been reading an account of Tasmania, which sounded a rather horrible country; there was a vivid account of a great bushfire which swept whole townships out of existence and nearly ruined any number of farmers—mainly by its destruction of livestock.[34] I don't think I'd care to live there.

I can well imagine how exhausting mission life must be, and can also see something of its compensations: my

---

34 The 1967 Tasmanian fires, also known as the Black Tuesday brush fires, burned over 652,000 acres of land in southern Tasmania. These fires injured over 900 inhabitants and killed 62 people in only five hours.

grandfather, a Church of Ireland parson, used to describe missionary work as "either the noblest of callings or the meanest of trades".[35] Which I guess, as regards the latter part, is no longer true; I suppose (and hope) that the trader disguised as a missionary is a figure of the vanished past.

I don't know enough about the contrasted scenery of Papua and Tasmania to imagine how the difference would strike you. I know when I came home after three years in China, it was the difference of colour values that impressed me most.[36] I remember standing on a south coast cliff on a bright summer day, and when my companion asked me what I thought of it all, I told her that my chief impression was the faded colouring—the pale blue of the sea, the wan looking grass and foliage. She replied with astonishment that the colour was brilliant, and of course a week or so later I would have agreed with her; but at the moment the whole scene to me was just a big faded tapestry.

As I think I said before, I'm all in favour of the closest collaboration between the various churches in that large field of work which they have in common; but no "watering down of belief". And union without such a watering down seems to me to be an impossibility. I am not prepared to abandon (or adopt) belief to which I stand uncommitted by

35 Lewis's maternal grandfather was the Reverend Thomas R. Hamilton. He served as rector of St. Mark's Church in East Belfast from 1878 to 1900.

36 Lewis's first tour of duty in China was from June 1927 to February 1930.

my Godparents and my own Confirmation vows.[37] To take the most important of all points—Communion administered by anyone other than an ordained priest of my own Church would not be a Sacrament at all, but a mere ritual commemorating the Last Supper. Of the Seventh Day Adventists I know nothing except the name; but how the Salvation Army, which I understand does not believe in any Sacraments, can unite with us is more than I can understand. In fact I don't get as far as understanding what such a Communion means. I admit that the ritualistic differences between C. of E. High and Low Church are very wide, but after all they both believe in the same essentials.

1911, 1921, and 1964 have been the outstanding summers of my lifetime—and of course in 1921 I had to find myself serving in West Africa, getting leave in 1922, one of the worst summers on record in England![38]

With all best wishes, yours sincerely, W. H. Lewis

---

37 The syntax is a bit tangled here. Lewis is asserting that he is not willing to add to or subtract from the vows he took when he was confirmed in the Church of England.

38 Lewis served in Sierra Leone from 1921 to 1922. At this time, he was a captain. The summer of 1922 was one of the coldest summers in British history. The average temperature in July was just 57 degrees Fahrenheit (13.7 degrees Celsius).

## 7

### Trinity
### 2 June 1969

Dear Major Lewis,

We seem to have a habit of writing at Festivals! You at Easter, I at Trinity. Thank you for your Easter good wishes; my Easter was happy and lovely indeed. My sister and I worship in Hobart's beautiful little St. David's Cathedral, which is a nice medium homely-cum-dignified sort of Churchmanship.[39] Incidentally, on Low Sunday they began to use the Series 2 Liturgy as an experiment.[40] I think I like it. I left home in that week, and your letter was forwarded on (or rather, back) to me as I returned, as I was staying in Brisbane with our

---

39 St. David's Cathedral in Hobart is the principal Anglican church in Tasmania. It was Biggs' home church, and her important work is commemorated there.

40 The text for worship, weddings, baptisms, and other Anglican services is contained in the *Book of Common Prayer*. In the mid-1960s, three "Alternative Series" books were produced, giving churches new options in both the structure and the language of service. These were met with some controversy.

beloved Archbishop Strong. He always welcomes members of his former staff as they pass through. While I was there he left for the Philippines and South Vietnam for the consecration of a Bishop in the former and to visit the Australian troops in the latter.

I hope you will not mind: I have posted you a book on New Guinea which I hope you will enjoy and find profit from. It is really produced for use in schools, but is clear, comprehensive, and almost up-to-date. I cannot fault its accuracy so far as my knowledge goes, but it has more to say about the New Guinea side than the Papuan. Now that you have unkind things to say about Tasmania, I almost regret that I did not find a book to enlighten your ignorance about that part of the Commonwealth!!! Tasmania is really lovely, and supposed to be more like England than any other part of Australia; but of course, it has lots more sunshine than England. You must not condemn it for its one disastrous fire; the effects of it are still there, though the forests (called 'Bush') are sprouting again in most areas, and new houses have sprung up to replace the old. The scientists have thought up a most ingenious way to prevent these fires in the future; they drop lighted matches that burn with an intense heat for one minute, in ordered paths from aeroplanes, during a time of no-fire danger. These burn the low scrub only, leaving the trees unharmed, and so form firebreaks which will prevent fires from spreading when the fire danger is high. If you want to know something of Tasmania (and Australia generally) much of what Anthony Trollope wrote in the 1870s is still true.[41]

---

41 Anthony Trollope's *Australia and New Zealand*, published in 1873.

When I first came to Papua 20-odd years ago, Bishop Strong was violently opposed to any trading for the same reason as you quote, that some missionaries had traded and earned a bad reputation thereby. Some Missions had founded their work on such an income. We are now swinging round to the conviction that we must trade to support our work. Voluntary donations from England and Australia are no longer enough to keep the work going, and that policy has bred a disastrous attitude among some of our people that the white man has plenty and can continue to run his schools and Hospitals at no cost to the Papuan. We are now trying to get the local people financially involved in supporting his own Church, and also trying to keep our financial heads above water by earning money in legitimate industry. In fact, our Secretary who is a very wise man, says that if we hold land and do not use it to its full potential (by growing copra, coffee, etc. etc.) we are being false to the Territory and its people who need all the urging by example as well as otherwise to develop their own country.[42] There is not much danger of our indulging in dishonest or unfair trading.

I have read of the brilliant colouring of China, though I have never been there, nor am likely to go; I loved England's colouring which maybe was not as striking as some countries.

I agree with you that the essential beliefs of our Church must not be watered down; but I think that much of our difference lies in emphasis rather than contradiction. I would be quite ready to receive Communion according to another rite, and even if it were a commemoration conducted by a man

42 Copra is dried coconut meat, from which coconut oil is extracted.

not ordained according to our ideas, I would not feel a hypocrite if I partook, believing that it was no more than a commemoration, and not giving it a value that it did not deserve. Maybe that would be an example of 'going the second mile'. There has so far been no example of that in New Guinea nor Australia—i.e. that people have been asked to do it in that way, all our co-operation so far has been in fields of worship that all could with a clear conscience unite in, and in co-operation in social, medical and other fields. This year our C. of E. men are training to be teachers at the Lutheran Training College, with an Anglican chaplain available; we are running one school in partnership with the Roman Catholics, and another in partnership with the United Church (Methodists, Congregationalists, and some other Protestants). It seems to be working well, and does witness to the New Guinea people that we are partners, not rivals.

My goodness, I do run on! But all that was inspired by what you said. I am off to Lae tomorrow for my last Standing Committee meeting, as Conference will appoint a new one in a few weeks, so now I must stop and do some 'homework' for it.[43]

With good wishes to you and your work

---

43 Lae is the second-largest city in Papua New Guinea. It is 164 miles (265 km) from Biggs' station in Popondetta.

## 8

23 June 1969

Dear Miss Biggs,

You will think I've been a precious long time in getting round to answering your interesting letter of Trinity Sunday.

I have only just got back from a wonderful month in the Isle of the Saints (in dull matter-of-fact English: Ireland), and one of the few good rules I never break is that <u>no mail</u> follows me when on holiday.[44] Ireland was as always a restful joy; living as I do in a now industrialized bit of England, you may get some idea of what it means to find yourself amongst a people to whom enjoyment of the simple things of life is worth far more than cash, a country where everyone puts fun before wages, where long hours are worked so slowly that work itself becomes a relaxation. Even the numerous donkeys seem to enjoy almost unlimited leisure and even when carrying home panniers of turf, do so with a slow deliberate gravity. And on a more serious level, how refreshing it is to live in a country

---

44 Lewis and the Millers left on May 27 for their annual summer holiday in Ireland.

where weekly church going is taken by all classes as—at its lowest level—a social duty. Sunday afternoons are the great sporting days of the week, but when you see a coach notice of an excursion to a Sunday football match, it will say "break for Mass at X Church, 10 a.m." What would an English football crowd make of such an interruption in the serious business of the day! By the way, congratulations on your admirable phrase "Homely-cum-dignified Churchmanship"—an ideal description of the ideal form of worship in my opinion. I am out of sympathy with all forms of Low Church, if for no other reason than because of their fanatical hatred of the Cross; and as for the Anglo-Catholics they strike me as *plus royaliste que roi*, more Roman than the Romans.[45]

I'm greatly looking forward to the arrival of the Papuan book, a thing I cannot always say honestly about books from pen friends. I have two in the States, one of whom bombards me with 'Flying Saucer' literature, whilst the other is trying to convert me to her belief in re-incarnation. Do you understand these people? It seems obvious to me at any rate, that if after death you return to earth as a different person, then reincarnation is simply another name for extinction. My correspondent's answer to that one is that ultimately I will be re-absorbed into the Divine existence—surely this again is that I–me—ceases to exist at all?

I was greatly interested to read of the swing in opinion on the subject of missionary trading, and from what you say there seems to be an unanswerable case for Missions entering

---

45 This phrase *plus royaliste que roi* can be translated as "More royalist than the king."

the commercial field—always supposing that they remember that they are missionaries first and traders second. But as you say, there is little scope these days for the old style bogus missionary exploiter. By the way I'm sorry to see you are a dollar country as otherwise I'd have liked to send your Mission a trifle—is there any agency in England to which I could send a trifle in <u>sterling?</u> My £50 I'm allowed to send into the dollar world has already been used up.

I started out to answer your letter and as usual have managed to write a letter of my own; but it is too late to do anything about that now!

With all good wishes, yours, Warren Lewis

## 9

29 July 1969

Dear Dr. Biggs,

How very kind of you to send me this interesting book, which I am reading with great interest, though still far, very far from being able to "sit" the examination papers at the end of the volume! I am so ignorant of the whole locality that I hadn't realized the administrative divisions of this huge island, nor did I realize that the natives were of different races. One thing I had heard about before was the cargo cult, which if my memory serves me, was talked of on a TV programme some time ago; but I think it cannot have been in your country, for so far as I can recollect, it centred on an abandoned World War Air Base.[46] Certainly the country looks beautiful in many parts, but then so did West Africa! Birds of passage used to go

---

46 Cargo cults are religions that rose out of the wreckage of World War II. Natives of the South Pacific believed that the Europeans and Americans obtained their power and wealth from the cargo they received. They believed that if a certain ritual was performed, cargo would be sent to them as well.

into raptures about Freetown, seen from the ship—the only pleasant place from which to see it by the way. And I notice that in places anyway you have my old friend the *anopheles* mosquito.[47] I remember too, in West Africa how tedious I found the division of the year into wet and dry seasons; and no doubt you long as I used to do for the familiar spring, summer, autumn and winter.

Now we should do our bit towards solving the ever-present problem of the balance of imports and exports. Cannot you think of some book published in England which you would care to have? If so it would be a pleasure to me to send you a copy.

Nothing has been talked about, televised and wirelessed about, reported on except the lunar landing and I tell you as a secret that I'm getting very tired of the subject. Of course I admire the courage of the men who made the great journey, but was it worth the billions—or is it trillions?—of dollars which it cost? When one thinks of the famine and misery which that money might have assuaged, one just wonders.[48] Only second to this as a topic of conversation is the Kennedy business, and as we are never likely to hear the truth about that, I feel speculation is a waste of time.[49]

---

47 *Anopheles* is a genus of mosquito prominent in the transmission of malaria.

48 Apollo 11 landed on the moon on July 20, 1969, and the Apollo 11 mission is estimated to have cost 355 million dollars.

49 Lewis is referring to the death of Mary Jo Kopechne. On July 18, 1969, Kopechne was riding in a car driven by U. S. Senator Edward "Ted" Kennedy on Chappaquiddick Island, Massachusetts, when the

More interesting to me is the fact that we have had a summer—seventeen whole days of it! But very heavy rain yesterday and today. Dear old England of course regarding all this as phenomenal and totally unready for it. We are an amazing people you know—every year we have at least one heavy snowfall and either flooding or drought; and public and the authorities alike regard it as something which has never happened since this island first rose out of the Atlantic. This time for example 17 dry days led (about the 10$^{th}$ day) to water being rationed in many of our big cities.

Ungracious though it may sound, I'm suffering from a spate of visitors, nearly all American, who gate-crash here to say they have been inside the house where "the gre-ate C. S. Loois" wrote. They seem to regard me as the custodian of a national monument, open to visitors daily 10 a.m.–6 p.m.! But bless them, it is something to know that interest in my brother is still so common.[50] And after all I've had a wonderful, carefree holiday in my own Ireland, and am going to the Suffolk coast for a fortnight in the autumn, so really, I have little excuse for grumbling.

With all best wishes, yours sincerely, Warren Lewis

---

car went over the side of a bridge and plunged into a channel. Kennedy swam away from the vehicle, but Kopechne was drowned. Kennedy did not report the incident for nine hours. Later, he pleaded guilty to the charge of leaving the scene of an accident. As Warren Lewis predicted, the details of the Chappaquiddick incident are still disputed.

50 The Lewis brothers' home, The Kilns, continues to welcome visitors. It is owned and managed by The C. S. Lewis Foundation in Redlands, California.

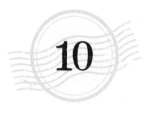

# 10

3 August 1969

My dear Major Lewis,

This correspondence has come a long way from the discussion of writing books which began it. I am too busy these days to think of writing except as a far-off dream; certainly not until I retire. I had serious thoughts about retiring after the present term of service, but our canny Bishop has given me a new job as Diocesan Medical Co-ordinator, and it is like creating a new portfolio; there is a fair amount of organizing to be done. I can't foresee handing over to someone else in less than four or five years, so long as I have health and energy to keep at the job, so the Bishop will have me for longer than I planned, and my nice little cottage by the sea is fading into the future. The Administration plans to close this Hospital at the end of next year, but so far has not come up with a sensible answer as to the disposal of the patients. The Administration bears the cost and the Mission staffs it. Then the Public Health Department would like me to be a peripatetic medical officer looking after tuberculosis patients throughout the North Coast of Papua. I think that the Director is not being very realistic about it; sick patients still have to be nursed!

Your holiday in Ireland sounds delightful; other people who have been there love the country too. Of course, you would look on it as your home. Have you relatives or friends still living there? I must confess that the news lately has shown up the Irish in a bad light, with their fights and riots on religious matters.[51] It takes centuries to live down old injustices and prejudices. But our hustling cities are creating a bad kind of society too. Our Papuans are infuriating in their failure to value time, but in our more sober moments we realise that they have values that we have not. They rarely suffer from high blood pressure, coronary disease etc.

You have some odd correspondents; flying saucer fans, re-incarnation enthusiasts and whatever I may be! It is a great temptation for anyone to try and convert their friends to their own pet belief. I imagine you would be pretty resistant to any sort of propaganda! I would love to 'convert' you to a love of my beloved countries, Papua and Tasmania; but part of me realizes that the way of the converter is unpopular and sometimes silly.

Our Diocese is praying for and trying to attain some degree of spiritual renewal; our Christians are in many cases second-class ones (and not only the Papuans). Some of our thinking is based on the renewal that occurred in the Diocese

---

51 Northern Ireland endured a series of bitter riots and confrontations in the fall of 1969, initiating a tumultuous period known as "The Troubles."

of Coventry.[52] We have a married couple working here as
A. V. A.s (the Australian equivalent of the English Volunteer
Service Abroad) who are very Protestant Protestants.[53]

We are trying to help us all spiritually and to grow in
Christian love by having weekly Bible Study classes. They are
not my line of country at all, but anyway we are all trying.
After a rather unfruitful study of St. James' epistle we have
now come on to Joy Davidman's *Smoke on the Mountain*, a
book that I have read and admired several times. We seem
able to build more on her than on St. James!

Basically of course, spiritual renewal must depend on
prayer, and one has so little time and less energy for it. Life
has been full to the brim of activity in the past three months,
very interesting but very wearying.[54] Today is the first day

---

52 The revival at Coventry Cathedral was a spiritual movement that
swept through the Anglican church in the late 1960s and early 1970s.
It was characterized by an emphasis on personal faith, prayer, and
evangelism, and it sparked a wave of interest in charismatic renewal.
Bishop Stephen Verney wrote about the experience in a book called
*Fire in Coventry: How Love, Prayer, and the Holy Spirit Completely
Transformed a Congregation*.

53 Australian Volunteers Abroad was established in 1963, and the first
teams were sent to Papua New Guinea, the Solomon Islands, Tanzania,
and Nigeria.

54 Some of Biggs' activities during these months included a special
meeting of the Medical Committee, a trip to Popondetta for another
administrative gathering, and the Diocesan Conference. She also spent
a week in Port Moresby for the double purpose of coordinating with
the Bishop in her role as Diocesan Medical Coordinator and organizing an upcoming conference for the Combined Churches' Medical
Council.

when I have declared war on "jobs" and determined to be social—on paper.

If you will forgive my curiosity, I would love to know how the Gresham boys are faring.[55] There is little mention of them in the book you edited about your brother, but I see he dedicated[56] one of

[*The text breaks off here, then resumes.*]

not bound to it, I am glad to say. However, we have an organization in England working for us. The Secretary is Rev. [Edward] Kelly, Secretary, New Guinea Association, 32 King's Orchard, Eltham, S.E.9.

What delightful names England has! King's Orchard makes me think of a King-of-Hearts person, complete with golden crown, casually picking apples and eating them.

I have been extravagant lately; I used some of the money from my sister's legacy[57] (she died two years ago) to buy a stereogram with radio.[58] It runs off batteries when the generator is not running, and off the electric power when available. It is a great joy, and I have some good records from here and there.

---

55 "The Gresham boys," David and Douglas, are Joy Davidman's sons. C. S. Lewis named them as beneficiaries in his will.

56 Biggs is likely referring to *The Horse and His Boy,* one of the Narnia books. It was dedicated "To Douglas and David Gresham."

57 Biggs' sister Lillian (known as Lil) died in 1967.

58 A stereogram is an audio system that includes both a record player and a wireless receiver. These are fairly large pieces of furniture, incorporating two large speakers set into a large wooden cabinet.

Now I am having pricks of conscience in case I have been too self-indulgent! Lord, what fools these mortals be![59]

    With all good wishes,

---

59 Biggs is quoting Shakespeare's *A Midsummer Night's Dream* Act 3, Scene 2, Line 121.

## 11

28 August 1969

Dear Dr. Biggs

What a pleasant surprise it was to open your magazine and there to meet you, if not in the flesh at any rate by camera.[60] I cannot say that I found the articles to be "simple" in the sense of being written for simple reads; to me they were just well-written and informative. I enjoyed them. I'm afraid the Papuans are not amongst the best looking races of the world if Daugi and Tago are fair specimens—"manly" is about the kindest way in which I can refer to their appearance! The political issue is of course beyond me.

I have also to thank you for a letter dated 3rd of this month, which was very interesting, though I'm sorry to see you in such an unsettled state. To an outsider it looks rather like a case of "too many cooks." Anyway I hope and trust that the whole "tohubohu" (delightful and self-explanatory French

---

60 Biggs had sent Lewis a magazine from the Anglican Mission that included an article and photographs about her work in Papua. There is no trace of this magazine or the handwritten note she included with it.

word!) will sort itself out to your satisfaction.[61] To get on with the job in a period of re-organization is one of the hardest things I know.

Yes, my poor Ulster is passing through a bad patch, but I've seen many such before.[62] The tragedy is that Protestant and Catholic are, one can say, <u>born</u> hating each other. I'm 3rd generation Ulster on my father's side and on my mothers, 5th; I've lived out of Ulster for fifty years; and the other night when I saw on Telly the Protestant boys marching and heard the band playing "The Boyne Water" I felt as if I could throw a bomb with the best of them.[63] Of course I said an instant prayer for forgiveness, but if I can react like that, imagine what the uneducated living cheek by jowl with their detested neighbours must be like! A sad, sad business.

We can sympathize with each other over our correspondents, but I'm one worse off than you, having in addition to a flying saucer lady, and a re-incarnation one, a spiritualist. All Americans, of course. The one I find the silliest is the re-incarnationist whom I've tried in vain to make see that if I'm to return to earth as say an Australian bushman, this is

---

61 The French *tohubohu*, meaning confusion, disorder, or chaos, is borrowed from the Hebrew words for "formless" and void," as used in Genesis 1:2.

62 Lewis is most likely referencing the Battle of the Bogside in Derry, Northern Ireland, August 12-14, 1969.

63 Lewis had strong Ulster unionist sympathies, identifying with Protestants who wanted Northern Ireland to remain within the United Kingdom. "The Boyne Water" is a moving Ulster folk song that commemorates King William III of Orange's victory at the Battle of the Boyne.

only one way of saying that for the me of today, death ends everything. Why not be an atheist which is much simpler and boils down to the same thing? But should you be interested in any of these the fascinating (?) subjects let me know and for Christmas I'll send you a small packing case of books about them!

One great thing about retirement is that you do have the time for prayer but alas, not always the inclination; but one must stick doggedly to a routine and pray for inclination. My plan is to get up at 6 a.m., make a cup of tea, then pray while the whole world around me is quiet. I've long ago given up the almost universal habit of saying my main prayer last thing at night—about the worst hour one could choose, I think.

I'm glad you like *Smoke upon the Mountain* which my brother thought highly of both before and after he met Joy. You ask about the Gresham boys for whom I'm glad to say I've no responsibility, they both being over 21. Douglas, the younger one is now a farmer in Tasmania and appears to be making a success of it—married to a nice girl (English) and with two children.[64] The elder boy, David, is something of a problem. He is a strict orthodox Jew, intelligent, with no vices, but who at around the age of 28 has never earned a penny in his life, though he works hard.[65] He is just back from a year at Jerusalem University and is now in England where

---

64 Douglas Gresham (1945-) and his wife, Merrie, currently live in Malta where he works as a voiceover artist, announcer, and film producer. They have five children.

65 David Gresham (1944-2014) became interested in Judaism in his teenage years and remained committed to the faith.

instead of looking for a job, he is about to enter Cambridge University—to study the Talmud and Arabic! He inherited about £6,000 from a grandmother and it is I suppose on this that he has lived ever since. But even £6,000 does not last forever, and what then? We are all troubled about him, but he himself is as unconcerned as if he had inherited £6,000 a year!

"Electric power when available" sounds a chancy way of life. Where does it come from and why isn't it always available? But then you don't have a dry season so far as I remember— just damp, wet, and very wet!

In case you have any curiosity about what I look like I enclose this snap. I'm the old gentleman in glasses and the other is my houseman.[66] It was taken at a village on the Suffolk coast where we sometimes borrow a cottage. We go back there for a fortnight at the end of next month. I don't expect you have gorse in Papua—the lovely rich golden wild stuff at our backs.[67]

With all best wishes, yours, Warren Lewis

p.s. My next job this morning is to send my Pensioner's Mite to Mr. Kelly.[68]

---

66 "My houseman" is a somewhat ironic/playful reference to Len Miller. Len and his wife Mollie were long-time neighbors on Kiln Lane. On April 17, 1967, the Millers moved into The Kilns and provided company as well as practical help to the Major.

67 Gorse is a thorny evergreen shrub native to Western Europe and Northwest Africa.

68 Lewis's financial support is in response to Biggs' suggestion of financial need mentioned in her letter dated August 3, 1969.

# 12

4 September 1969

My dear Major Lewis

I would have written before but I have been fiercely busy, partly on my own two jobs (TB & Leprosy Hospital and Medical Co-ordinator) and partly organizing a Combined Missions Medical Conference to begin on the 12th September. I shall resign the Secretaryship. Now, however, I have acquired an "inflammation of the supraspinatus tendon"—fibrositis to the non-medical world –which makes every movement of my right upper arm very painful.[69] So I am typing more or less with my left hand, being unable to do other jobs more urgent. I even have to let the girls on the staff help me dress, do my hair, etc. Tomorrow I am to go to my colleague 7 miles away for an injection into the tendon of Cortisone which (I hope) will produce magic results.

Your letter with the photograph arrived last night; thank you

---

69 The supraspinatus muscle runs along the top of the shoulder blade; the supraspinatus tendon continues across the top of the arm. Inflammation of the muscle and tendon is usually caused by overuse.

so much for it. It makes you look rather different from the photos in your book. You look a remarkably young 73! Is your "houseman" a man who looks after your house—the masculine form of housekeeper? My only knowledge of the word is for a young doctor doing his residence in a Hospital for experience!

I am familiar with gorse; some of the early

Warren Lewis. Photo from the Marion Wade Center. Used with permission. Note that the actual photo does not accompany the letter.

Tasmanian settlers must have brought it out from home and it grows beside some our roads, much as it is in your picture.

My schoolgirl French did not extend to the "tohubohu," which I think must be the equivalent of the local language's "tepotapo" and Wedauan's even more expressive "lubalababa."[70] Our own "higgledepiggledy" is the nearest I can get, which also is good onomatopoeia.

After a lot of painful trial & error, I have come to the same experience as you, that bed-time is the worst possible time for prayer. I also am lucky in that I do not have to be on duty early. The nurses go on duty at 6:30 a.m., but I not till

---

70 Wedau (also called Wedaun or Wedawan) is a language local to the Oro Province.

after breakfast, so I start my day at 6 with a cup of tea, then prayers, then dress and get ready for the day. So we are alike in that. On Sundays and Thursdays we have Communion at 6:30, so private prayers get shelved somewhat. A really good Christian would wake ½ hour earlier, but not I. Our friars put me to shame with their life of prayer. Did you know the Franciscans at Cambridge? I believe that your brother used to visit them sometimes.[71] Bro. Michael was at Cambridge for many years, and he visited us about 1956. The Friars are a real support and help to us in countless ways.[72] We know also that when we can manage it, we are welcome to visit them for a quiet weekend, and with a little or a big Q, as we please.

You ask about our electric supply; it runs off a generator on an engine, and we run it at stated hours. We have a 30 horse-power one here which supplies our lights, domestic power, sterilizers, and hot water systems (luxury for missionaries!).

Please do not send me a packing case of books on spiritualism etc.! It would be quite an unfriendly act! When there are so many interesting things to read, why worry about what appears to me to be rubbish or fraud, but I am possibly biased. Certainly I am willing to believe that there is communication between the living and the dead, but I believe it much as I

71 Biggs may be thinking of the Oxford Friars. There was a religious community in Oxford called The Society of Saint John the Evangelist (SSJE), founded in Oxford in 1866. These friars, especially Father Walter Adams, had a significant impact on C. S. Lewis's spiritual formation during the 12-year period from 1940-1952.

72 The Society of St. Francis began their ministry in Port Moresby in April 1959. They established their Novitiate in Haruro, near Popondetta, and worked closely with Biggs and her sponsoring organization.

believe in angels; and I do not expect to meet either a spirit or an angel round the next corner. Have you read J. B. Phillips's book? (I thought it was in *Your God is Too Small* but I can't find it there); anyway he says he saw your CSL a few weeks after his death sitting in his room watching television.[73]

But I must confess to some curiosity about your own books, of which you have said almost nothing. I must confess that my knowledge of the world of books is very limited, but I have never seen anything under your name. Perhaps you use a nom-de-plume? If your books are on military strategy, of course none of them would come my way. If you are very anxious to help restore the balance of trade that I think would be a delightful way of doing it. However, I have so little time for reading that it might be months before I could manage to read it.

No magic results yet from my injection, but I have had less pain for which I am truly thankful.

My sympathy to you in being treated as a custodian of your own home. Tourists are a menace—but nevertheless I change my view rapidly when *I* am the tourist. I hope you continue to greet them graciously for a Christian duty; I am certain that I would not. I hope that your holiday in Suffolk will be very pleasant, weather included, and blessedly free from tourists! I really hustled up this answer so that you would receive it before you left home, as you do not have mail forwarded. I shall not have a spare minute in the coming weeks. I am selfish enough to hope that my arm will prevent

---

73 This story is told in *Ring of Truth: A Translator's Testimony* by J. B. Phillips. Phillips (1906-1982) was a canon of the Anglican church.

me from taking Minutes at the Conference that I can without being ungracious pass the job to someone else. But we expect great things at conference, medically and spiritually. So far we have about 35 coming; half are [Roman Catholic], 1/3 United Church (Protestant bodies) 5 Anglicans, and a couple of Lutherans. What would Ulster say? Poor Ulster, it is very sad. It does look as if British police are the best answer to the rioting.[74]

Thank you for your information about the Gresham boys; I might even meet Douglas some day in Tasmania. I have the reputation of being un-curious, but with you I am quite the reverse.

These air-letters are annoying because one's space is limited, but they are much cheaper than a proper letter by air.

With good wishes,

---

74 There were riots August 12-17, 1969 in Northern Ireland. Irish Catholics marching for civil rights were attacked by Ulster Protestants and the Royal Ulster Constabulary. There were eight casualties and many houses lost in the resulting fires.

# 13

15 September 1969

Dear Dr. Biggs,

Many thanks for yours of the 4th which I enjoyed in spite of the bad news. I, thank God, have so far no experience of fibrositis my own much easier crosses being rheumatism and lumbago; both painful and a handicap, especially the latter, but not I'm told to be mentioned in the same breath as fibrositis.[75] I do hope the injection will or rather now *has* brought you relief and that the trouble is permanently banished. It has at least the small compensation of relieving you of the tiresome business of recording minutes at the Conference.

A houseman (the term is imported from America) is not exactly a housekeeper but her partner and complement. In my case he drives the car, does the garden, and is dexterous and does the hundred and one odd jobs which crop up in a house—replacing broken tiles on the roof, repainting a room, coping with electric failures and so forth. He is in fact just as much an indispensible member of the household as is the

---

75 Lumbago is pain in the lower or lumbar region of the back.

cook/housekeeper. All blessings upon them!

Though your 6 a.m. and mine are no doubt at very different times, it gives me much pleasure to think of us both boiling the kettle and settling down to prayers at our own six a.ms. No, I didn't read the Phillips book (*Ring of Truth*), but the relevant portion was reprinted in our *Parish Magazine*; and I know something about the author who was a correspondent of my brother's.[76] There was nothing of the conventional ghost about the appearance; in the author's own words my brother "was ruddier in complexion than ever, grinning all over his face and positively glowing with health". Phillips adds that it did not occur to him to attempt to touch him and suggests that his reluctance to do so may throw some light on the appearance of the risen Christ.

I fancy that all my books are out of print; at least they have long ago ceased *paying* anything. You wouldn't care for them unless you are interested in 17th century France (the only subject I know anything about). I've got a spare copy of one of them, and if you think you would really read it I'll get it off to you as a Christmas present!

I see I've missed the information that you have already had the injection with no magic results; which I'm very sorry to hear, but let us hope that it will bring about a gradual improvement.

Yes indeed, poor Ulster; and now two soldiers have been killed over there. There will be devil and all to pay over that,

---

76 Lewis copied the article from *Parish Magazine* and wrote a brief comment on it in his journal on Thursday, December 5, 1968. He concludes, "To me the whole episode brings very mixed feelings."

both in Ulster and in England.[77]

with all good wishes, yours sincerely, Warren Lewis

---

77 Lewis is referencing Operation Banner, the name for the British Armed Forces operation in Northern Ireland, which started as he was writing in 1969 and concluded in 2007.

# 14

26 October 1969

My dear Major Lewis,

I expect that your autumn holiday is now over. Holidays need fine weather and I hope that you had it, with trees ablaze with their autumn colouring. I have never seen England at that time, except in pictures, and in Tasmania one sees it only where English trees have been imported. I wonder if you do much walking now? If you have kept up the habit, you might still indulge in what is usually a young man's hobby.

Our conference went off very well, and, as we were meeting in Port Moresby where the Administration has its seat, we felt that our numbers were impressing the powers-that-be.[78] We all think we should have higher subsidies and more help from the Government and when we meet thus we can impress them more forcibly. The Director spoke to us about a new scheme of subsidy which should be an improvement. As it is, they pay an inadequate amount for selected members of

---

78 Port Moresby is the capital of Papua New Guinea; it is also its largest city. It is located about 90 miles southwest of Biggs' home base.

our staff, both white and brown, and supply drugs on a fairly rigid basis of variety and amount. A Mission doctor draws a subsidy of $1400 per annum (= £700) which is paid to the Mission, and what the Mission pays that particular doctor is their own affair. Because TB Hospitals are on a different basis, the Govt. pays a subsidy for me equal to what they would pay one of their own doctors doing this job: viz, $6000 or thereabouts. Of course I draw the same allowance from the Mission as my colleague who draws only $1400. As Missions do a large proportion of the medical work of the Territory we feel that we should receive more. The rest of the medical costs come from the pockets of our supporters. The Papuans have just begun to pay a very small fee for medical service, which is meant to introduce them to the idea rather than to help the financial situation.

We found that we could worship happily in one another's mode and there was a very good spirit among us. We stayed in a Roman Catholic staff house; as we Anglicans could not get to a Communion service of our own, we attended the Roman one and were welcome there. One morning our Devotions were taken by Bro. Andrew an Anglican Franciscan who is also a medical student; the next by the R. C. Archbishop of Port Moresby; the next by a group of Protestants. It was altogether extremely good. I have handed over the job of Secretary to a doctor of the Plymouth Brethren persuasion.

You ask about our languages: New Guinea is reputed to have anything from 400 to 600 different languages, with dialects and sub-dialects.[79] The *lingua franca* of Papua is Police

---

79 There are now more than 800 known languages in Papua New

Motu, a simple corruption of the Port Moresby language, and through the New Guinea part of the Territory Pidgin is the rule. This varies of course, but has a German element, thanks to the Germans who ruled here before World War I. The British and Foreign Bible Society have just published a Pidgin Bible which was prepared by many Missions working together.[80] God is rendered as "big-fella-long-sky" or some such horror. However, they say it is an elastic and expressive language and is better than our Motu.

17th century France is an unexpected study for you to have made your own, but probably a most interesting one. I always regret that I did not make history my hobby if not my study, but I know little of France of that time beyond what I learned at school in European History. If you would care to send me your spare copy (provided that it really is spare) I could at least remedy some of the omission.

Last week we had our Hospital Festival on St. Luke's day; I was here only for the early service which was really very good.[81] We invite old patients who live near enough to come for Church & breakfast. A number of the staff from our sister Hospital, St. Margaret's, walked the seven miles before 6:30, which was pretty good. Then our priest and his family and I

---

Guinea, many of which are spoken by only a few hundred people. However, English is quickly gaining prominence in the biggest cities.

80 *Buk Baibel long Tok Pisin*, or *The Holy Bible with Deuterocanon in the Tok Pisin* (Melanesian Pidgin), compiled by the Bible Society of Papua New Guinea and published by Faith Comes by Hearing in 1969.

81 St. Luke's day is on October 18. Luke is the patron saint of physicians, surgeons, and doctors.

had a quick breakfast and went off to Dogura by Cessna air-craft for the opening of a new Administration block of their Hospital, St. Barnabas'.[82] Dogura is our Cathedral Station and very lovely. They have just lost their doctor, an English girl who came out to relieve me when I had a trip to England in 1964, and stayed on. She felt that she must resign, and we are sad to lose her. I went down to see her patients and sort out some TB problems down there. I do enjoy running round in small aeroplanes; do you? This country of course could not function without them. We did the trip in 70 minutes that would take 3 or 4 days by coastal boat. There is not and could not be a road between us.

My arm got rapidly better, thank you. Good for Cortisone. I wish it could be of benefit to your rheumatism, which probably is much harder to bear than my very localized pain. However, the doctors shy clear of Cortisone for these long-standing things.

We lose our Secretary in a few days; she is handing over her job to a Papuan she has trained for it. She goes to England for a long leave of absence, including a term at Selly Oak.[83] We will miss her badly and the patients still more. She is the one who mothers them.

It is now time for the "sched" when we talk to each other from hundreds of miles apart by radio. Now we have it, we wonder how our Mission ever functioned without it. We can also talk to other Missions during their scheduled times if necessary, as we all use the same wavelength.

---

82 Dogura is a mission station in the southeast of Papua New Guinea.

83 Selly Oak is an area in the southern part of Birmingham, England.

I hope you are not freezing yet! Maybe you like the cold? With good wishes,

# 15

11 November 1969

Dear Dr. Biggs,

Many thanks for your letter of 26th. October. The holiday was delightful and the amazing weather has continued almost up to the moment. On 1st of this month we had a wireless announcement that October had been the driest October for *two hundred* years and the warmest for a hundred—two records I'm hardly likely to see broken![84]

I was interested by your account of the Conference, but scandalized at what you tell me about conditions of pay—specially when I think of my neighbours in the car plants drawing around £2,000 a year for a 48 hour week with fifteen days fully paid holiday a year—plus casual holidays such as Easter, Christmas and so on.[85] It is all part of the absurd, indeed wicked idea that priests, doctors, hospital nurses and

---

84 October 1969 saw 0.66 inches (17mm) of rain. The average rainfall in Oxford is around 2.55 inches (65mm).

85 At the time, Oxford was a major automobile manufacturing center, due to Lord Nuffield and his Morris Motors.

so on should have a soul above such sordid considerations as money—or to put it more realistically, that they should accept the fact that their employments are sweated labour — and this in spite of St. Paul's insistence that the labourer is worthy of his hire—adequate hire I presume he meant.[86] I do hope you will be successful in getting your finances put on a more up to date basis.

What you have to say about getting on with other denominations makes pleasant reading, and I only wish my own unfortunate Ulster could acquire the same spirit. But I doubt if anything of the sort is even in sight. Too much history— and inaccurate history at that—is the curse of my part of the world and the result is that Protestant is born hating the Catholics and vice versa. It's all very sad and apparently quite ineradicable.

Bible translation is a ticklish problem, isn't it? I remember once seeing a version for Eskimos in which "lamb" was translated "little seal." It read very oddly—"Oh little Seal of God that taketh away the sins—" But after all, what else could you say? No good talking to an Eskimo in terms of some animal he had never set eyes upon.

My interest in 17th century France began in the most humdrum way. I was in 1919 stationed near St. Omer in Flanders, and went in one day to hunt for something to read—came across an abridgement of the memoirs of Saint-Simon, bought it, liked it and continued to collect similar books—of which

---

86 In I Timothy 5:18, Paul writes, "the labourer is worthy of his hire" (ASV), echoing the words of Jesus found in Luke 10:7.

today I've got around 500.[87] I'm sending you a copy of one of my own ones and hope you will like it—though goodness knows when it will get to Papua—perhaps it will serve as a 1970 Christmas offering?

I haven't done any flying since the 1920s when I used to be taken up by the Air Force in the open cockpit machines of those days. I liked this but don't think I'd care for the modern plane—certainly the air liner which looks to be about as interesting as a bus trip. But my dear R. C. nuns who operate in Africa and fly their own plane give me most enthusiastic accounts of the joys of flying.

I'm delighted to hear that the arm is better and thanks to the wonderful weather I'm free, or nearly free, of rheumatism. But I'm afraid winter will soon alter that state of affairs!

With all best wishes, Warren Lewis

---

87 Louis de Rouvroy, duc de Saint-Simon (1675-1755), was a French diplomat. His memoirs are extensive, and they are considered a classic of French literature. In 1964, Lewis published his own abridged and edited edition of *The Memoirs of the Duc de Saint-Simon*.

# 16

7 December 1969

My dear Major Lewis,

I am developing a mental picture of you, incomplete in some respects, but each letter fills in a bit more, and your photograph. I fancy that there is quite a good deal of Irish in you—more than there was in your brother? You seem to spring into an anti- or pro- frame of mind more readily than a slow person like myself. You did rally to the cause of underpaid overworked doctors etc.; of course we are missionary doctors etc. supposedly supported by our Churches at home, and I think the Government, rightly or wrongly, think they are being most generous in helping us at all. However, the home Churches do not and probably cannot give on the scale needed to run educational and medical services; so the Mission makes do with what she has. However, Australian wages rise so often and so high that the cost of living swings higher and higher; so that what was formerly an adequate rate of pay for missionaries is now quite inadequate. Our Australian Board of Missions decided at its last meeting that they would somehow find the money to raise our allowances. I am lucky, as my family legacies give me a few extra dollars per year, but those with absolutely no resources are harder hit.

We are living in the middle of a fairy-godfather story, but, alas, it looks like falling flat. My dear Nance Elliot with whom I have been working fairly closely for all our 21 years here, and who is in the category of "no resources at home", has just had a most wonderful offer of a trip overseas next August, round the world, including Oberammergau—and even including a day at your beloved Oxford!—with even spending money included, from an anonymous donor.[88] Dear Nance whose conscience is like a lump of Scots granite, says she can't accept "charity", and that the money ought to be given to the starving people of the world. The Bishop passed on the offer and commented, "You must accept this; no one deserves it more". I tried to persuade her till I thought again. Anyway she has written to a priest of the Franciscans whom she trusts for understanding advice, and there the matter rests. But it all brings up the somewhat thorny question which many of us face in a smaller degree. Our friends at home know that we are poorly off (in money matters anyway) and often present us with a cheque or a few dollars "just for yourself, my dear". It is often welcome, and it is certainly generous, sometimes involving even more sacrifice on the part

---

88  Nancy A. Elliot was a trained nurse from Melbourne who worked with Biggs from 1948 until Elliot's resignation in 1971. She was also an accomplished seamstress, establishing a sewing center in the late 1960s to teach the Papuans how to sew garments and supplies for the clergy and churches within the Diocese. Biggs was very fond of Elliot, rarely referring to her without a complimentary epithet.

of the donor: but there is often a feeling of humiliation in accepting it, and not being in a position to give something in exchange. Nance is a born giver, and spends her life in giving her work, her ideas, her intercessions, her sympathy, and her money in greater quantities than she can spare, yet she hesitates about accepting this. I do not know myself whether the unwillingness to accept is a sort of pride or an attempt to keep one's integrity. I would be interested in your views, if you have ever been in a position to form any.

I will look forward to receiving your gift of your book, anyway; no pride bound up in that! I do hope I can find time to read it soon. Most of my reading is done in bed when I am sleepy, and yours is not that sort of book—or it would be a poor sort of compliment to treat it thus. For that reason I have been over 12 months reading the fascinating *The Bible as History*—have you read it?[89] It is the sort of book one could read many times; and now I am longing to read some extracts from Josephus, which I have in a paper-back. Reading is like an infectious disease!

My brother was in Northern France and Belgium in World War One; it played havoc with his nerves for years but he has settled down into a contented citizen now.[90] Last year he paid a visit to the old battle-fields, and could even identify a trench where his friend was killed, a farmhouse where

---

89  *The Bible as History* by Werner Keller was first published in 1955. This book includes scientific and archaeological evidence in support of the Bible's authenticity.

90  Biggs had two brothers, Reg and Len, who both served in France and Belgium during World War I.

he had been billeted, and met on a bus the son of a woman who had billeted him—and was enthusiastically embraced by this Frenchman to the entertainment of the whole busload of passengers. His memory is very clear of the terrain. The woman who billeted him had a daughter who later married an Australian soldier and lives in Victoria; my brother, who also knew her in France, has kept in touch with her. As it all happened in Armentieres, this woman is treated as, and may even be, the original of "Mademoiselle of Armentieres", which no doubt you have sung, even if you are not an Australian![91] However, you may not have been in that part until after hostilities ceased.

You will surely have begun your winter weather now, and I fear that that may mean a return of your aches and pains. We are having our usual December weather of very trying heat and humidity with really impressive thunder storms beginning. When I sweat and try to keep cool I must think of you piling on your woollies and putting more coal (?) wood (?) on the fire.

I hope that your Christmas will be a blessed one. I know that mine, whatever it may be, will be a busy one!

Yours very sincerely,

---

91 Armentieres is a town in northern France. Biggs is referring to a song popular during the war.

**17**

19 December 1969

My dear Dr. Biggs,

Many thanks for yours of the 7th. I wouldn't say I'm more Irish than my brother was, for he had a warm and lifelong love for our native County Down, one which I share with him.[92] I'd be inclined rather to attribute the difference to the fact that he had not only a much better brain than I have, but also one more given to weighing up the pros and cons of a situation. But he would certainly have shared my feelings about underpaid and overworked people in your field. The trouble about giving is the commonplace one of—to whom? Is it better to give all you can spare to one object, or to spread the butter pretty thin over as many objects as appeal to you? I try to be as generous as possible to as many as possible, but hold that such cases (individual cases) as are personally known to me are my No. 1

---

92 County Down is one of the six counties of Northern Ireland. In a letter written to Arthur Greeves, C. S. Lewis remarked, "You know that none love the hills of Down (or of Donegal) better than I." (*Collected Letters* I:330).

priority. Would you say I'm right?

In the case of your friend this, like nearly all questions in life by the way, is one which only she herself can resolve. But if she was my friend I should ask her to consider very carefully whether her efficiency as a worker in her own chosen field would not be increased by the benefit accruing from this holiday. Looked at from that point of view no one could—she herself could not—regard the holiday as an act of self-indulgence or even as mis-spent money. But I fear that if she is, as I suppose, a Scot, she will have already made up her mind and will not be persuaded to change it even by the Franciscan. I've often been up against this charity complex myself and know how hard it is to overcome it. No doubt it is more blessed to give than to receive, but giving is a sight easier than receiving. Time and again I've had the experience of knowing that someone is desperately hard up and the only way I've been able to give them money is by inventing a job of work for them; then the money becomes not charity but payment for value received (even if the "value" is non-existent) and the money can be accepted. This brings me back to the question of institutional plus individual charity. For the first there is this great advantage, that you escape the net of the professional beggar; I've a long familiarity with the latter class, for my dear brother was not only the most credulous of men, but also used to say that he would sooner give to one he thought a fraud rather than risk refusing a genuine case.[93] I saw

---

93 C. S. Lewis wrote, "It will not bother me in the hour of death to reflect that I have been 'had for a sucker' by any number of impostors; but it would be torment to know that one had refused even one person in need" (*Letters to an American Lady,* 108).

his point, of course, but could not conceal my opinion that his policy did not make the best uses of his resources.

What an amusing and touching story that is of the *rencontre* on the bus![94] Yes indeed, I once knew Armentières as well as I now know Headington.[95]

It would be idle now to wish you a happy Christmas unless I added "in 1970". But at least I do wish you a happy and blessed New Year.

Yours very sincerely,

Warren Lewis

---

94 *Rencontre* is an encounter between two persons.

95 Lewis served in France from November 1914 to April 1919. Headington is a suburb of Oxford, where the Lewis brothers' home, The Kilns, is located.

# 18

1 February 1970

My dear Major Lewis,

It is indeed a late time to wish you a happy New Year! But I do hope that 1970 will be kind to you. Your letter arrived on Dec. 29th, which was quite quick. Our January has been a terrible month, maybe the hardest month I have had in this service, and personal affairs just had to be shelved. We seem to be emerging from the worst of the depression. But this letter may well be a short one, or else a means of letting off steam; neither of which is very kind to you.

Your question about the method of giving what money one can is rather hard for me to answer; I suppose your plan of spreading the gift over as wide a field as you can is the best; I am such a partisan-type of person that I get just a few interests and try to help the few along as generously as I can. Of course in this country we are not exposed to the numerous appeals of civilization; any gift involves the writing of a letter or sending a cheque.

My Nance decided to accept the gift of a tour; and our

Franciscan friend used much the same arguments as you did, and added that she should accept it as a gift from God, even though it comes through a person. She is now beginning to find joy in the idea. You are quite right in saying that it is harder to receive than to give, when the medium is money or goods; when it is time or service the giving is sometimes very hard. When money is given, it is certainly a protection to the individual if the money is given to the institution he (or she) represents. But I suppose there are temptations even then. When does life not present us with temptations?

I have not been sleeping very well with the recent worries and have been reading in sleep-time more of Charles Williams. I have Mrs. Hadfield's *Introduction to Charles Williams* and also one of his novels.[96] It is a pity that such reading is of necessity superficial; I am too tired to do more than skim over his thoughts and ideas. He must have been a wonderful friend. I am just coming up to the Oxford part. Your book, by the way, has not arrived yet. I think the Post Office puts mail on the first ship leaving for a destination regardless of its expected time of arrival. Several of us received Christmas cards last week that were posted in England in early November.

I suppose you have noticed that if anything goes wrong, everything else goes wrong as well? Staff affairs have been worrying in other parts of the Diocese (and come back to me as the Coordinator) and then this Hospital blew up into one of the common epidemics of wrong-doing. Our patients stay

---

96 *An Introduction to Charles Williams* by Alice Mary Hadfield was the
first full-length biography of Williams.

here for about two years or sometimes more, so that they are uprooted from their homes and village disciplines. We try very hard to train the staff to respect the patients and keep the medical-patient relationship healthy. Of course sexual misbehaviour is fatal to that and there are few Papuans who can say No to any sexual temptation. I have made a rule that any member of staff so misbehaving must be dismissed at once. I found out two weeks ago that every one of our single male staff had been visiting one girl, who was under the legal age of consent anyway. The leader of them was our Papuan Secretary, and without him I simply cannot run this Hospital. I handed over the problem to the Bishop, and all of us were glad that he upheld the rule and sacked the lot—including one nurse who had been organizing the gang. But he said that the Secretary and cook must stay on until new staff could be found and he is trying to get a volunteer from England to take over the office. Another nurse went off in sympathy, so our purely medical staff has been reduced from 13 to 3. We are managing somehow and getting in new staff who will have to be trained, of course, as fast as we can.

I must say that our Bishop is a wonderful person to work with; we are very lucky in our Bishops. His predecessor said in a similar, but not so bad, situation, "At least, when things go wrong, you know what the devil is up to; when things go right, you are just left wondering <u>what</u> he is up to!" It is easy to believe in the devil here; and it is also easy to believe in guardian angels and the grace of the Holy Spirit. The sad part of all this upheaval is that the dismissed boys are such nice lads, maybe the nicest we have had. But the devil got into them and we are all paying the price of it.

Now I have let off steam to you; I hope you do not mind. It is now dinner-time and the evening is booked up, so I must finish this letter.

With all good wishes,

# 19

10 February 1970

Dear Dr. Biggs,

Many thanks for your kind letter of the 1ˢᵗ.

I'm so glad to hear that your friend has accepted the trip and of course her view that it is a present from God must be the right one; after all, the giver must have been inspired by God to give, so it amounts to the same thing. If to receive is harder than to give, it is on the other hand a better thing for the soul is it not? Reception must involve something of humility, giving is a constant temptation to pride. I speak feelingly about this because I've just done a considerable financial service to a dear friend and was horrified to find myself telling myself that after all I'm a pretty good sort of a chap aren't I? *Retro Sathanas!*[97] By the way I wonder can you tell me what to say to the folk who when approached for money by missionaries, reply that charity begins at home and anything

---

97 *Retro sathanas* may be intended to evoke the words *vade retro sathanas* ("Get thee behind me, Satan") spoken by Jesus as recorded in Matthew 16:23.

they can spare goes to the relief of poverty in England? It may of course be an excuse for not giving to either, but the particular case I have in mind I know the donor is a sincere and generous Christian.

Yes, Charles Williams <u>was</u> a wonderful friend and one of the very best men I've ever met in addition to being a very brilliant one. Oddly enough I'm re-reading one of his novels myself at the moment with that care which the job demands; for no one could describe Charles as an easy author. Did I ever tell you how his friendship with my brother began? Each wrote the other a fan letter and the two crossed in the post![98]

I'm very sorry indeed to learn that you are depressed and not in too good health—for to sleep badly is one of the most trying forms of ill-health I know and none the less so because sound sleepers regard you as a *malade imaginaire* who is making a great fuss about a trifle.[99] I suffer from it occasionally and find the only remedy barring drugs which I will not use, is to get up, brew a cup of tea, smoke a cigarette and then back to bed. Under these conditions I often turn a bad night into a fairly good one.

But no wonder you are troubled after this upheaval in the Hospital and the loss of the secretary must be a serious matter

---

98 C. S. Lewis wrote a letter to Charles Williams on March 11, 1936, expressing unabashed enthusiasm for Williams' novel *The Place of the Lion*. Williams replied the next day: "If you had delayed another 24 hours our letters would have crossed" (Lewis, *Collected Letters* II:184). Williams had been reading the manuscript of Lewis's *Allegory of Love*.

99 *Malade imaginaire* is French for "imaginary illness." The phrase was popularized when it was used as the title of a 1673 comedic ballet written by Moliere.

and put a great deal of extra work on you. I see of course that your action was the only one you could possibly have taken, but speaking generally I've never been able to summon any great degree of moral indignation over sexual offences—of course provided that they do not entail disaster. It must I'm sure have struck you that Our Lord denounces sins of the spirit much more severely than those of the flesh—as for instance in the case of the woman taken in Adultery, or the other woman in Samaria with whom He had the conversation at the well. But perhaps here there is a divergence between the male and female view of this particular sin.

I like the sound of your Bishop and he must be a tower of strength to you all. As regards the new address the "free mail bag" intrigues me. Does it mean you don't have to pay postage when you use it?

With all the best and my hopes that your troubles will soon sort themselves out,

Yours sincerely, Warren Lewis

## 20

17 February 1970

My dear Major Lewis,

Your book arrived ten days ago, not long after I had written saying that it was slow in arriving. So did some other English mail posted at about the same time. It must have come on a tramp ship wandering the globe! Well, it was well worth waiting for and I am very pleased indeed to have it; and hope soon to read it. For some reason, I expected it to be largely figures, dates, and statistics—possibly because of your military background?—but it looks very human. And the publishers have done a very handsome job in producing it. Thank you so much.

I still don't know if it was right or wrong of me to pour out my troubles in your last letter. There are so many people one cannot pour them out to, and you and my sister [Win] seemed to be a sympathetic and uninvolved ear to besiege. Things are improving, both as we collect new staff and as the morale improves. I think everyone is resolved to be very, very good—until Satan gets a new attack going!

I'm off to Dogura, our Cathedral Station for the weekend, mainly hunting up TB patients; then on to Port Moresby for a few days to see the Public Health heads, and other officials connected with the work. It will be a pleasant change, even if it is not a holiday. I like flying in little Cessnas; the one we use is just like a little motor car with a couple of wings attached.

I must not stop for more, but I did not want to delay any longer letting you know that your gift had arrived.

With all good wishes,

# 21

24 February 1970

Dear Dr. Biggs,

I'm very glad that the book has at last come into port after its Odyssey through the Seven Seas; but I think from its travels I would be ill-advised to send you a box of hot cross buns for Good Friday!

I am very glad to find you in better spirits than when you last wrote and hope that you are now out of the wood. But be assured that if you care to unburden yourself to me, you will find a sympathetic even if unhelpful listener.

Two nights ago I saw a Papua travelogue on Colour TV and naturally it interested me on your account. Everything was on a larger scale than I had pictured it—gorges deeper, enclosing hills higher and so on. All who saw it were in raptures about its beauty—and of course it is beautiful; but I noted the wisps of white cloud over these steep forests climbing up from the river bed and reflected that I know exactly how beastly it would be to climb up there! One shot I found horrible—a native girl who was obviously in great pain, having her back tattooed with what appeared to be a blunt nail driven through a piece of wood. And the hideous ceremonial costumes of the men—ugh!

A friend of mine is wintering in Hawaii and sends me photos of the native men and women there, from which it seems to me—don't throw bricks—that the natives up there are much further removed from the savage than are your Papuans. Hawaii men are fine looking fellows and the girls are, even by European standards, pretty.

I've nearly been betrayed into writing a letter where I intended only a couple of lines of acknowledgement of yours. The result is that I have written neither!

Must be off now to keep a tryst with my dentist.

With all best wishes, yours as ever, W. H. LEWIS

Palm Sunday
22 March 1970

My dear Major Lewis,

I hope that this will reach you in time to wish you a happy Easter, but I expect not. But the good wishes are there. We will have our service at 6 a.m. (as we did this morning) and that is likely to be all the festivities we indulge in; though we might invest in some bacon for breakfast as some of the staff like it very much. On big Stations they sometimes have native dancing and a native feast. Good Friday is observed quite strictly by long custom in fasting till 3 p.m. completely, or else with only a drink. Even the heathen often observe this without any prompting. We also observe silence till 3, and people, including children, are very good about that. Of course Hospital routine demands a bit of whispering of reports, instructions etc.

You quoted the old "Charity begins at home" in your letter to me.[100] People do bring it out as the final instruction

---

100 That is, her letter from February 10. Mail delivery between the

in alms giving, but I wonder why? Who originally said it? It is not in the Bible. "Charity" in that context may well be the charity of Second Corinthians Chapter 13, and that would make it more meaningful than the sense that is usually made of it. I should think it ought to be (in respect of our gifts) "Charity begins where there is most need". That is where the Good Samaritan started.

Maybe it is as we grow older, either older in wisdom or older in Christian experience, that we become more aware of Satan's little underhand attacks at us. I am sure you are not the only one who finds himself, almost by surprise, patting himself on the back for some good deed. At any rate, it is good that one does become aware of them and can fight back.

And now to your book. I began it after my return from Moresby, but have decided I must abandon it until after Easter for some more appropriate reading. Knowing that you and your brother wrote such imaginative things as boys, I wonder that I ever expected your writing to be statistical and unimaginative. You must have had a lot of fun reading up all these old records, letters, etc., and then breathing your own kind of life into them. It makes excellent reading, even though I am not far into it yet. (I told you I was a slow reader).

You, like your brother, seem to sit light to sexual offences, and I think you may be right that women view it somewhat differently from men. It may be a heritage from the Victorian prudishness that would be kept alive by the women, but even that in its turn might have arisen from (a) the need of a

---

continents was unreliable. While these letters are arranged chronologically here, they were not always received in an orderly fashion.

woman for security in marriage affairs; and (b) concern for the illegitimate children. And in this country a woman's pregnancy is so often the first evidence of misbehaviour, and it is rising to dreadful proportions, so that one is forced to take it more seriously than one would at home. In many districts as far as one can tell it has all begun since the coming of the white man with his more permissive ways. One of my lads said to me, "It is all the fault of you Christians; you told us we must love each other, and so we did!" The barrier of language (and European misuse of the word love) crops up everywhere. They are not in a position to understand your brother's "Four Loves"![101]

I am glad you saw a travelogue on Papua; I wonder what part? It does not sound like our Anglican area, although we have some magnificent mountains. Tattooing is going out of fashion a good deal, and the type and degree has always varied from tribe to tribe. Nearly always they are tribal markings. More often it is the women rather than the men who are tattooed, but in the Managalas mountains behind here the men have some very fine designs over trunk and limbs, as well as face.[102] Our people don't make much fuss about the pain, I

---

101 In *The Four Loves,* published in 1960, C. S. Lewis defines and describes brotherly love, maternal love, romantic love, and friendship.

102 New Guinean tribal tattoos usually depict animals and other natural objects, which are thought to bring spiritual support to the bearer. In some societies, women are not seen as suitable for marriage until their bodies are covered in the tribal patterns of their female predecessors. The most common technique of tattoo application is to cut open the skin with a thorn and pour pigment into the wound. Pigments are obtained from various sources, including seeds, roots, and battery

believe, though I have never seen it done. A girl occasionally has the name of her boy-friend tattooed on her arm by her own wish—and quite often changes her mind and after her marriage to another the old name remains, of course. They usually do it with a thorn, sharp and fine. But I agree with you that other parts of the Pacific have had civilization longer and maybe were more readily adapted to it as well. In our country you can find every type of man from complete savage with cannibalistic habits to a suave man with a University degree who can hold his own in any English circle. But the latter are not often found.

This Diocese, in common with many others, is trying to introduce a new Liturgy. We have a Liturgical Committee that has been working on a Series 2 type of service, and then putting it into still simpler English for our half-educated people.[103] None can use it until the congregation has a copy to use and study, so duplicators are working on temporary copies. The Friars, as usual, head the field, but our District is to try it out soon. It is all very good; but I often find myself wishing that our modes of worship could stay put so that we could get on with our praying instead of adapting to new ways. A sure sign of advancing age, I fear! But at least I have it in common with your brother. He mentions it in *Letters to*

---

acid. As missionaries to the region gathered cultural influence, they increasingly discouraged such traditions.

103 In the mid-1960s, the Anglican church began a period of designing alternative services to supplement the Book of Common Prayer. One result was the publication of *The Alternative Service Book,* intended to offer alternatives to the BCP but not to replace it.

*Malcolm.*[104] I suppose that Malcolm was a real person?
With all kind regards,

---

104 C. S. Lewis, *Letters to Malcolm, Chiefly on Prayer.* This book is written in the form of letters from Lewis to a friend he calls Malcolm. In the first chapter, C. S. Lewis explains that the ideal church service is one "we are almost unaware of; our attention would have been on God" (4). One key to achieving this ideal, according to C. S. Lewis, is that the liturgy would be free from innovation, staying "always and everywhere the same" (4).

## 23

4 April 1970

My dear Dr. Biggs,

Your welcome letter of the 22$^{nd}$ March was very nearly on target as it reached here on the 1$^{st}$. of this month.

I'm very surprised to learn that the heathen in your parts observe, or at any rate seem to observe, Good Friday. Can it be that the day falls about the same time as mourning for some heathen god? Unlikely though, for at that season one would expect heathen to be rejoicing at the kindness of some fertility god or goddess. We had a very good Easter here in [Headington] Quarry—Communions at 7, 8, 10 and (choral) 11, all well attended.[105] I took advantage of my years to make mine at eleven and found the church very nearly full. But I've never really adjusted myself to this service after years of going to the 8 a.m. Indeed I'm rather ashamed to confess that I get more good from a sparsely attended service "when two or

---

105 Holy Trinity in Headington Quarry continues as a thriving church. It is less than a mile from The Kilns.

three are gathered together."[106] But I'm quite wrong of course, one ought to wish for a crowded church.

I don't know who first began the "charity begins at home." I can't and don't think Corinthians very helpful in support of it. Somewhere or other St. Paul urges <u>special</u> doing good to "those who are of the household of Faith" but it is difficult to square this with "charity begins at home";[107] it would be applicable only if those at home were of the household of faith, and alas, this is very far from being the case![108] As I think I told you before (we old men repeat ourselves) my problem about charity is quite a different one, and purely practical. You have, say £100 to give away; do you do most good by sending one worthy object the whole hundred, or by sending twenty worthy objects £5 each, or by any larger divisions of the £100, say between four objects? Ethical considerations are not involved; you have bestowed £100 in charity whatever course you follow.

I think that all men "sit light to sexual offences" for the regrettable reason that there is not one man in a hundred over twenty-five— "queers" excepted of course—who has not been guilty of several sexual offenses; whereas until the collapse

---

106 Matthew 18:20: "For where two or three are gathered together in my name, there am I in the midst of them" (KJV).

107 Galatians 6:10: "As we have therefore opportunity, let us do good unto all men, especially unto them who are of the household of faith" (KJV).

108 Lewis may be thinking of Janie Moore, who lived with the Lewis brothers from July 1930 until her death on January 12, 1951. She was an atheist, and her critical and demanding nature caused Warren Lewis distress.

of all morality which began in World War One and is still spreading, there probably was not one woman in a hundred of our social class who <u>had</u>.[109] Today I'm told that the most virtuous girl is not in the least offended by a man's proposal that they should spend a weekend at Brighton as Mr. and Mrs. Smith—though she will of course decline the suggestion with thanks! But after all, should we not, women and men alike, show more indulgence to sexual sin? The greatest Man who ever lived seems to have regarded it more indulgently than other sins; "the woman taken in adultery"[110] was spoken to in very different terms to those used towards the Pharisees;[111] and—to translate into modern terms—He showed no anger when a prostitute broke in upon him at table and spent a bottle of expensive Beauty Aid upon Him.[112]

I think it must have been the Managalas country I saw on

---

109 The use of the term "queers" is likely to be intended as descriptive rather than pejorative. Lewis probably shared his brother's view, expressed in the radio broadcast of *The Four Loves*, "How a man can feel anything but bewildered pity for the genuinely homosexual I've never been able to understand."

110 This story, recounted in John 8:1-11, concludes with Jesus declaring, "Neither do I condemn thee: go, and sin no more" (KJV).

111 See, for example, Matthew 23:27: "Woe unto you, scribes and Pharisees, hypocrites! for ye are like unto whited sepulchres, which indeed appear beautiful outward, but are within full of dead men's bones, and of all uncleanness" (KJV).

112 This story is told in Luke 7:47. The Pharisees were disgusted by the sinful woman, but Jesus tells a parable and concludes by saying, "Wherefore I say unto thee, her sins, which are many, are forgiven; for she loved much: but to whom little is forgiven, the same loveth little" (KJV).

TV because there were several men with magnificent feather headdresses and they had the whole of their faces tattooed. Interesting what you say about female marks because we had something of the same kind in West Africa.[113] A betrothed girl had a tattoo mark on her thigh indicating this fact, and when we got out there we were warned that if we caught playing the fool with a girl so marked, authority would make no effort to protect us from the consequences of our folly! Native men who tried it were, if I recollect aright, subjected to an operation by the witch doctor which rendered them incapable of ever repeating the crime.

I'm pleased to hear that you at any rate propose to read my book and am only sorry that it isn't a better one. I like it least of any of mine.

I'm very tired of all this messing about with the Liturgy and my Roman Catholic friends tell me that they are suffering in the same way. It is of course quite a different thing to produce something simpler for native consumption, our versions being often quite unintelligible to them, not only of the Liturgy but of the Bible—hence the very odd sounding (to us) invocation in the Esquimo Bible "O Little Seal of God…" No use talking to an esquimo about lambs—he wouldn't have a clue to what you meant.

No, there never was a real Malcolm.

With all best wishes, yours sincerely, Warren Lewis

---

113 Lewis was stationed in Freetown, Sierra Leone, from March 9, 1921, to March 23, 1922.

## 24

26 April 1970

My dear Major Lewis,

"O to be in England
Now that April's there"[114]

I wonder if you are having a lovely Spring? We are busy entertaining our Queen (ours as well as yours) with autumn colours in Canberra.[115] I fancy that England welcomes back the light and sunshine and some degree of warmth with a great sigh of relief. Here we are very late changing from wet to dry season; even on Friday the Popondetta airstrip (grass) was closed because of heavy rain the night before. They say it takes 4 inches of rain to make it too sodden for use. But Popondetta also has a tarmac strip left from the war which it also uses.

---

114 These are the opening lines to "Home Thoughts from Abroad" by Robert Browning, written while he was on holiday in Italy.

115 In 1970, Queen Elizabeth II toured much of Australia, accompanied by Prince Philip, Princess Anne, and Charles, the Prince of Wales.

Maybe I gave you the wrong impression when I said that the heathen observed Good Friday. When they are alongside the Christians they merely follow suit with the fasting and silence. They observe no anniversaries of their own in their native state; they have a special day for hunting, planting gardens, dancing, etc., but there is always a village "old man" to appoint the day and it has nothing much to do with the calendar.

It is good to know that Oxford is still interested in its religion, on Easter Day anyway. I agree with you about preferring a service of "two or three" for the same reason; also because I prefer a said to a sung one—especially here where the singing is pretty hard to bear. One can still long for a crowded Church and not be inconsistent in wanting a quiet service, I suppose. Just as I am all for ecumenical services with all sorts of odd customs, rites and what-have-you but I would much prefer to go myself to plain Evensong.

Your problem about giving away money, whether a little amount to several charities, or one big gift to the lucky one, is usually decided by one's natural bent, I should think. As you say, there is no ethical problem; and one must just accept that, whatever one does, someone will benefit and someone else will not. My own natural bent, I think, would be to spread the gifts over a number of good causes, partly because it spreads the interest: it might give one more contact with interested people and a casual discussion of that particular good cause might stimulate other people to give who otherwise would not. But that is all theoretical. I must say that the thing that comforts me most is when my friends write and say, "I remember you in my prayers regularly"; it is worth many gifts of money as a morale-booster! And then I have to own to my shame that I find little time to remember in prayer those who pray for or help me.

My beloved Nance Elliot is beginning to get ready for her trip overseas.[116] She leaves on July 31st, and leaves Australia about August 14th. She plans to have an extra ten days in England instead of returning home via America. I suggested that she might call and see you on my behalf if you were agreeable, but she is a very shy person; and also she might well not have the opportunity. She "visits" Oxford with the tour people on September 15th, but as she also sees Windsor Castle in the afternoon, time will be very short. She might get back to Oxford in her extra ten days; I don't know. She and Irene (our former Secretary) hope to have a day or so together at Iona, and have a number of friends to see.[117]

On Saturday mornings we hear a BBC feature called "Profile".[118] Two weeks ago we heard your Irish Bernadette; she sounded much more mature than her years suggest, but her views were mixed up with a youthful approach.[119] Poor

---

116 Nance Elliot left Papua New Guinea for a lengthy trip overseas in the spring of 1970. She visited Oberammergau, Germany, and Oxford, England, among others.

117 Irene Beatrice Markham was bookkeeper and secretary of the Mission from January 1963 until December 1973.

118 The BBC "Profile" programme, still a popular radio show, offers an in-depth look at figures currently in the public eye.

119 "Irish Bernadette" refers to Bernadette Devlin McAliskey, an Irish socialist and republican political activist. She became a member of

Ireland; she just can't let the religious topic rest.

The Government has recently done a Survey for TB—a "mini" X-ray of all the population who can be got together. Then any whose little film is suspicious is to come to this Hospital for large X-ray, sputum tests etc.

I am supposed to get them in at the rate of 20 per week and it keeps me busy. Of course they don't come willingly as a rule and are only too ready to run off home before their investigations are complete. As my colleague has been on patrol and soon goes off for another week, I have his Hospital to keep an eye on as well as my own while he is away. The telephone is out of order that links the two Hospitals and transport is hard to come by, so things are not easy. His wife who is the Sister in charge wanted me at midnight last Tuesday; the creek was in flood so that she could not even leave the Hospital till it subsided. She got a member of staff to bring her up here on the back of his motorbike; found that the Eroro Creek half way was too much in flood for the bike; so it waited for her on one side while the jeep brought her the other 3 miles to see me at 2 a.m. She got my words of wisdom, which were to give some treatment and await events, and then the poor jeep-driver and motorbike owner could get back to their beds. We hope to have the phone repaired by next weekend.

O, I didn't talk about your book which I did enjoy. I

---

the United Kingdom's Parliament in 1969, at age 21, and served until 1974. The same year of her election, she was convicted of incitement to riot at the Battle of the Bogside and served a brief jail sentence.

think the duc du Maine may have had an osteo-myelitis.[120]
Must discuss it next time.

    With best wishes,

---

120 Louis-Auguste de Bourbon, duc du Maine, had one leg shorter than the other. Biggs suspects that the cause was osteomyelitis, a bone infection that causes disfigurement.

## 27

6 May 1970

Dear Dr. Biggs,

Many thanks for yours of April 26<sup>th</sup> which arrived yesterday—pretty good going don't you think?

"Having a lovely spring indeed"! It <u>began</u> yesterday and the winter that lasted until the 4<sup>th</sup> meant that we have been robbed of the early flowers which are to me what make spring worthwhile. But our grievances are so trifling compared with your hardships that I won't mention them again.

Interesting what you have to say about your people. In West Africa the natives were more sharply differentiated into Christians, Moslems, and the heathen, the latter taking their orders from the local "Juju Man"—and so I suspect did the Christians at moments of crisis! An odd thing happened last week—a retired Major whom I'd never met before came to consult me about a life of one of Louis XIV's generals which he is writing. In the course of general talk I discovered that he too had served in Sierra Leone—and that there we had both occupied the same bungalow!

I see that you, like me, are a plain old-fashioned Protestant, now a most unfashionable thing to be over here. "Choral Eucharist" as they like to call it, is all very well in a way occasionally when it is perfectly done in a Cathedral—but an attempt at it by the average village or suburban church is to me very painful. One of the things I'm most looking forward to in Ireland—I leave for there on Monday 11th—is the said services and specially the said Communion Service. But we must not deny others the sort of spiritual nourishment they find most appetizing. I knew a man once, a regular Communicant, for whom life was hard; he used to tell me that for him it would be impossibly so without the spiritual nourishment he got from the hymns!

I need hardly say that I shall be very pleased indeed to meet Miss Elliot if it suits her. But don't urge her to visit me. I know few things more annoying in a small way than the officious person who says "Oh so you are going to X are you? I've written to my friends the Ys and they will be on the lookout for you so be sure you call." Tell her to come only if she feels she would like to do so and has nothing more amusing on hand. You sound as if you would soon need a holiday yourself what with 2 a.m. calls and all the rest of it; if so I hope it will be England and not Australia.

Bernadette Devlin announces that she is giving up politics and would that Paisley did likewise.[121] I'm frightened of

---

121 Ian Paisley, a key religious figure and politician from Northern Ireland, founded the Democratic Unionist Party. Bernadette Devlin McAliskey continued to serve in Parliament until 1974, when she lost her seat to a Unionist opponent.

that man—heard him on TV the other night, and he isn't at all the buffoon I'd thought him. He is a rabble raiser of genius, another Hitler, and the hysteria he raised in a mob was terrifying—and this too, disguised as a <u>sermon</u> preached in a Church.

TB with us is not I think any longer a major problem, though it used to be when I was a boy. The real killers today are cancer and thrombosis.

God decided the problem of giving for me this year—an agonized appeal from <u>one</u> really deserving case absorbed all that I had to give!

With best wishes, as ever, Warren Lewis

# 25

Postcard Westport
14 May 1970

[Lewis to Biggs]

*From May 11 to June 3, 1970, Warren Lewis and Len and
Mollie Miller took their annual holiday in Ireland. The following two notes are handwritten on small postcards. This first
one features a photograph of the Aasleagh Falls near Leenane,
Connemara, County Galway, showing a small waterfall, green
hills, and a large, pink flowering shrub in the foreground. There
is no salutation.*

Here I am in the wilds of Ireland and reveling in it—and
pity you in your jungle. But alas, when this reaches you our
holiday will be only a memory. Only snag is a <u>Bank Strike</u> all
over Ireland which makes things difficult![122] As ever, W. H.
Lewis

---

122 Ireland experienced three bank strikes between 1966 and 1976. The
longest one, referred to here, lasted for six and a half months, from
May 1, 1970 to November 17, 1970.

# 26

Postcard Dunfanaghy
26 May 1970

[Lewis to Biggs]

*This postcard features a photograph of several homes clustered along the rocky coast of the Rosguill Peninsula with a blurb that states "Donegal is the most northerly county in Ireland extending along much of the north-west coast. It is famous for its scenery, with a beautiful much-indented coast, great areas of mountains, deep glens and many lakes. The Rosguill Peninsula in the north of the country is particularly beautiful and this entire district is an ideal holiday region. The circuit of the Peninsula by the 'Atlantic Drive' is one of the finest scenic roads in Donegal."*

For once in a way the blurb is right. We were round here yesterday and it is "one of the finest scenic roads in Donegal"— or anywhere else I know for that matter. And, I imagine, very unlike a coastal scene in Papua.

    With all best wishes, Warren Lewis

## 28

24 May 1970

My dear Major Lewis,

This used to be "Empire Day" (Queen Victoria's birthday) and it is strange how quickly history changes and Empires go out of fashion. I wonder how England celebrated it?

Your card came on Friday (22nd); how nice of you to remember me while on your holiday. A lovely view you chose, but the azaleas (are they azaleas?) were a surprise. Almost as if they did not belong. Your holiday has been very short; I expected you to be away a month or more, and that is one of the reasons why I did not write before. Another was that I have been very busy and my day off has found me without the energy to do the things I really wanted to do. I did want to say some more about your duc du Maine and the affection you obviously have for him. I found a book of famous lives recently (all women) and one was of Mme. de Maintenon.[123] It did damn her with faint praise! Following your St. Simon,

---

123 "Madame de Maintenon" is a name given to Françoise d'Aubigné, wife to King Louis XIV of France.

no doubt. It also thought little of the duc du Maine. My word they were a lustful lot, weren't they? Not enough else to do, I expect. Du Maine seems to have lived an amazingly virtuous life (in that specific sense) compared with everyone else.

I wonder how you organized the illustrations, both portraits and drawings? I don't imagine that you yourself asked permission of the authorities (Louvre?) to reproduce portraits etc. Maybe your nice agent did. And what about the cover design: Does an agent arrange all that, or does the author pester his artist friends to do it? It certainly is very effective. I am sending the book off to my sister (today with luck) so that she can read it too.

I am glad that your dilemma about giving away your money solved itself. I find that God usually points the way when one genuinely tries to find His will, even in matters like this which are not a choice between right and wrong.

I read the part of your letter to Nance that referred to her. Her comment was, "His answer was so delightful that I must try and visit him"—in short, you have won her from her shyness. I know that at heart she would love to visit you. We still don't know if it is going to be possible. She (and Irene Markham who may arrive with her) are both CSL fans, though they haven't had an opportunity to date to be WHL fans! By the way, my latest book purchase is your brother's Reflections.[124] I haven't had time to read it, or rather, my reading has been in lighter vein. I lent it to one of our priests staying with me, who said it is excellent, but not food for a

---

124 C. S. Lewis's *Christian Reflections* is a collection of essays addressing a wide range of subjects, including ethics, faith, and culture.

tired brain. Maybe I'll take it with me on leave.

My leave is due in October, and I gently reminded the Bishop on Friday. It depends on whether we can get a Sister to replace one leaving this week. I can't leave Jan on her own for too long without someone else to help. Jan herself is an A. V. A. (Australian form V. S. O.) and will be leaving us with her husband in January, alas.[125] I would have to be back before she left, to see her replacement settled in. We live by faith with a vengeance! A holiday in England would be wonderful, but it would have to be a summer one, and long enough to justify the cost of travel. With the fantastic rise in the cost of living, one doubts if it will ever be a possibility. Anyway, it is all in God's hands.

I would not class myself as a Protestant, if that term means the opposite of High Church (a term that is fortunately going out of fashion here.) I like (in fact, I love), a Choral Eucharist with all the trimmings, but if it is done badly, I would rather go without it. The same with hymns—I want 'em well done or not at all. As I had a somewhat "classical" musical upbringing, I am fussy. I wonder if you enjoy music as a relaxation? I have much joy from a record player and some records of the Bach, Beethoven, Schubert variety.

This is largely because my eldest sister [Bessie] and youngest brother [Oscar] were quite accomplished pianists and it was just part of my childhood to hear these things. My education in poetry was just what school affords and I feel it was cut short too soon.

---

125 Biggs is referring to two global volunteer organizations: the Action Volunteer Alliance and the Voluntary Service Organization.

Are Napoleonic wars the pet interest of retired majors? One can understand that they might well be. But even allowing for that, it is indeed a coincidence that people with that hobby should serve in Sierra Leone, and live in the same house! Did you ever by chance meet the Bishop of Sierra Leone & Rio Pongas?[126] I forget his name, but I met him when he had been translated to Korea. He did a wonderful job in Korea, so let's hope he did likewise in your part of the world.[127]

We are just changing over to a new kind of financial life. All these years the Mission has supplied our domestic needs and we have received a personal allowance only. As from July 1st we are to have a Mess allowance and run our own affairs. It coincides with a necessary rise in our personal allowance too. We had a meeting in Popondetta of Heads of Stations to be told of the new system. It is very good to meet all our old friends again from scattered Stations.

Must stop! Best wishes,

---

126 The Rio Pongas is a river on the west coast of Africa, about 100 miles (161 km) north of Sierra Leone. Both areas were included in the same diocese.

127 This is Bishop John Daly, who ministered in West Africa from 1935 until his transfer to Korea in 1956.

## 29

5 June 1970

Dear Dr. Biggs

Many thanks for yours of May 24th.

I don't think Empire Day is noticed any longer but as I was in Ireland at the time I can't say. How true a prophet Kipling was when he warned us at the height of our arrogance that the day might come when we were "one with Nineveh and Tyre"![128]

I'm so glad you found something to amuse an idle hour in the Maine story, poor man, he hadn't much chance with that she-dog of a wife of his, had he? As regards the illustrations, that is a matter for the publishers, though of course an author has a courtesy right to object to any of the publisher's suggestions. In this particular case, they had a lot of photos

---

128 Rudyard Kipling composed the cautionary poem "Recessional" on the commemoration of Queen Victoria's Diamond Jubilee in 1897. Lewis is quoting from the third of five stanzas: "Lo, all our pomp of yesterday/Is one with Nineveh and Tyre!/Judge of the Nations, spare us yet,/Lest we forget—lest we forget!"

sent over from Paris and left it to me to choose the ones I preferred. They did the cover design on their own.

You don't make it clear when you say "Reflections" whether you refer to *Christian Reflections* or *Reflections on the Psalms*—the former I guess, for the latter is easy and excellent reading whereas the former is by no means a bedside book.

I shall look forward to meeting your friend [Nance] if it proves at all possible, but I mean no disparagement to her if I say that I am even more anxious for a visit from you. Well, only mountains never meet and I shall live in hopes that your English leave in this year materializes.

As long as I was mobile I was a keen concert goer, but rather a heretical music lover, or so I've been told, e.g. I prefer Bach to Beethoven and Brahms to either; I'd sooner have chamber than orchestral music and in my opinion Debussy and Ravel have written better quartets than Beethoven ever did! As regards church music I quite agree; we for instance have a small, indifferent choir, yet the Vicar insists on a full Choral Eucharist every Sunday. The result so far as I'm concerned is that I never go to it at all, but make my weekly communion on Wednesdays when we have a said service and are literally "two or three gathered together." As for the hymns, the trouble as I see it is that all the music—well, nearly all—is so abominably cheap that it doesn't matter whether it is well or ill sung.[129]

---

129 The Lewis brothers were alike in their distaste for church hymns. C. S. Lewis has often been quoted as referring to hymns as "fifth-rate poems set to sixth-rate music" ("Answers to Questions on Christianity," *God in the Dock*, 61-62).

Ireland was out of this world as usual, but they too have their troubles. Cost of living is up 10% and what used to be the poor man's paradise is now more expensive than England—as I proved myself, for this year's holiday, identical with that of 1969 cost just that 10% more. And they are worried by an unexpected influx of wealthy German settlers of dubious antecedents who are behaving with typical German arrogance, treating the Irish as second-class citizens in their own country. Very unwise of them I think, because the Irishman when pushed too far is apt to protest against that kind of treatment with a shotgun. The annual American invasion they regard rather differently; they want the dollars but don't like the brash manners of all too many of their American visitors. The big surprise for us this year was climatic—temperatures of 48-9 degrees and old folk huddling over roaring fires in the hotel lounges [in Ireland] whilst in this country there was almost a minor heatwave. But we didn't allow this to interfere.

all good wishes, as ever, Warren Lewis

# 30

15 June 1970

Dear Dr. Biggs,

This is not a letter, but just a note to tell you of an amusing little incident yesterday (Sunday). Though in Oxford, I couldn't attend my own parish church and at the one I did go to I found I was to hear a missionary sermon. Well, in due course the visiting priest mounted the pulpit and said he was going to talk to us about "Papooa" (I never knew the correct pronunciation before). The acoustics were abominable, but as he progressed, he began to tell us of life at Popondetta and I pricked up my ears; but when he went on to tell us of staff shortages and praised the administrative services of Dr. Blanche Biggs, I sat up with a jerk!

If this had happened in my own church I would of course have made a point of meeting this man after service; but I felt I could hardly do this as a stranger. No doubt the Vicar wanted to hustle him off for lunch for one reason. But I did look at the church notice board when I was coming out and discovered that I had been listening to a Mr. Browning.

With all good wishes to the valuable administrator, sincerely, W. H. Lewis

## 31

28 June 1970

Dear Major Lewis,

Well, well. Dame Chance is a very odd person, if she contrived to get you to a different Church just when Fr. Denis Browning was to preach there! (We in this Diocese use the title Father, and it does describe the relationship between priest and people very well). I am so sorry you did not make yourself known. Fr. Denis is a man interested in all people (and as you will have noticed) has a great zest for new experiences, and I know he would have loved to meet you, not only for my sake, but also for your own. And if the brotherhood of Christians means anything, the Vicar could have invited you home to lunch with him! Or maybe that is an Australian (or Papuan) tendency rather than an English one. Fr. Browning (though we usually use Christian names with the title Father; and I am often Doctor Blanche) has been on the staff of the Martyrs' School for years and is having a year off now; when he returns at the end of September he is to be the priest in charge of our next door parish—and that is 8 hours away by boat, ½ hour away by air, and about 8 days on foot, crossing many crocodile-infested rivers. The Bishop has been here for our Diocesan Medical Committee, and may have to miss the next one because he will be installing Fr. Denis in his new work.

While on the subject of titles, I believe it is the English custom to call Army officers by their title after their retirement, and I have met one or two in Australia who used their title of Major. Or are you more often called just Mr.? In the same way I find that your brother was sometimes called Mr., sometimes Dr., and sometimes Professor. I do not think that in Australia one would ever call a Professor Mr., though one might refer to him as Dr. as he would be sure to hold a doctor's degree. My rude brother who was a Bachelor of Sciences used to tell me that he had as much right to the title Doctor as I had, as I am merely a double Bachelor; but then people will call a physician Doctor, regardless of correct procedures.[130]

Medical Committee was strenuous; we had six members staying in the house, but the job of feeding them fell on my colleagues, bless them. We went on till after midnight on Friday and for the last hour I was barely "with it", a bad thing as I am Chairman. The Bishop, bless him, kept alert and

---

130 Biggs graduated from the University of Melbourne in 1946 with a Bachelor of Medicine/Bachelor of Surgery, sometimes abbreviated MBBS. The designation suggests they are two separate degrees; in fact, they are awarded together upon graduation from medical schools that follow British academic traditions. The American equivalent would be an M.D.

followed a rather footling[131] discussion with courtesy. One thing did emerge; I said it was very doubtful if I would be able to get away for my leave, as the rest of the staff will be either coming or going; he said "You <u>must</u> have your leave", and I know he will do his best to get some more or less permanent staff to tide us over. But this leave could never be in England; I am not prepared for it; it is not worth while going unless for a long stay, longer than a 3-months leave; and I could not face the famous (or infamous?) English winter. My sister estimates that, if we go together in a year or two, our trip would cost $4000 (£2000) each—with costs still rising, as you found. But I do long to go again before I settle down to the life of a pensioner in a unit.

Committees and Budgets are so disturbing that I have not been able to sleep (don't worry, I'll make it up) and to take my mind off silly worries I have been turning to the Narnia stories, reading by torchlight. They are delightful and so wise.

Poor Ireland! She is in the news again today. I am sorry that your Bernadette is the cause of it. She is a far more attractive leader than the Protestant parson.[132] There seems to be no end to it all—unless the Irish combine to turn on the unpopular German element!

Thank you for the lovely view of Dooey (what a name!) and it is pleasant to think of you driving past those bays— by car? Do you take your own? It is a little like the N. W. coast of Tasmania, or would be if one could be sure of fertile

131 Footling means trivial or unhelpful.

132 The cause of the uproar was probably Bernadette Devlin McAliskey's determination to sit as an Independent Socialist in Parliament.

"paddocks" stretching back to blue mountains in the background. I am sorry the weather was so poor for you.

Yes, the "Reflections" I wrote of are the *Christian Reflections*. The borrower has not yet returned the book; I must jog his memory soon. I have read *Reflections on the Psalms* long ago, and, as you say, it is very readable.

I recently read a book on the Coastwatchers in New Britain during the war, and felt tempted to send it to you—maybe as a birthday present, as I fancy that your birthday is some time in mid-year.[133] But I hesitated to send it, as you might prefer not. Or you might prefer it as a loan? I suppose you keep your interest in things military, even the very informal and irregular guerrilla type of fighting they had to adopt. One of the main characters in the book was our District Commissioner up to two years ago.

I shall now think of you going to Mass (we say Mass, as it is simple) on Wednesday mornings, possibly at the time we are going to Wednesday Evensong and Preparation for our Thursday morning one. My mother used to do much the same thing—she would go on a weekday or an extra Sunday quiet service.

all good wishes,

---

133 The Coastwatchers were Allied forces stationed in the remote Pacific Islands to monitor Japanese activity during WWII. New Britain is the largest island in the Bismarck Archipelago of Papua New Guinea.

## 32

9 July 1970

Dear Dr. Biggs,

I thought you would be amused by this odd quirk of Dame
Fortune and am only sorry that the tale had no more satisfactory ending, but I could hardly have done what you suggest.
Hospitality in England and in Papua are two very different
things. Had the Vicar asked me to lunch you may be sure that
behind the Vicaress' smile of welcome a hearty Commination
Prayer would have been in full blast![134] Why? Alas, in this
tax-ridden and inflationary country, hospitality—specially by
those not over endowed with this world's goods, has to be
exercised sparingly and after forethought. I saw my butcher's bill yesterday and found that a pound of steak now costs
15/— and everything else is in proportion; indeed many what
used to be called "well-off people" have dropped butcher's
meat from the domestic menu entirely, and live on birds and

---

134 Commination is a type of prayer denouncing sinful behavior. The
Anglican *Book of Common Prayer* contains liturgies for Ash Wednesday,
which include Commination prayers.

fish—with of course the result that the price of birds and fish is rising rapidly.

Fr. Browning mentioned his new post in his sermon and commented with some heat on the condition in which his predecessor had left the parochial motor boat. I shall soon be quite an authority on the affairs of Papua, shall I not?

At our parish church we too use "Father" and "Mass", though I've never got quite accustomed to it, being as I think you know, a Belfast Protestant. If news of my unhappy native land has reached you, you will see what a dreadful time we are passing through over there, and over here it is not possible to give English people any idea of the crux of the problem. Take my own case. Most of my life has been spent in England or abroad and I severed my last links with Ulster when my father died 43 years ago. Yet when I saw a horrible interview on TV the other night with a Protestant woman, expecting her fourth child, whose husband had been shot dead at his own door for the crime of not being a Roman Catholic, I had a kind of brainstorm. I saw with savage joy a vision of the armoured cars going into action, heard the stutter of the machine guns, and saw the Catholic mob going down before them like swathes of ripe corn. I of course pulled myself together at once and asked forgiveness. But if I, an expatriate of 75, can feel like that, what is the use of talking peace to a community of the uneducated who have believed from their cradles that—according to the accident of birth—either all Non-Catholic will burn everlastingly, or alternatively that the Pope, if not himself actually diabolic, is at least the chosen vessel of the devil? No, it's hopeless unless we have divine intervention.

Many thanks, and I would indeed like to have that book if only as a token of your regard. Please write something inside it, and you can back date to my birthday, 16th June. It is kind of you to have thought of it.

Regarding titles, it is usual to retain the army rank for life with us, so Major is correct, but Dr., Professor, etc. are somewhat different. All men who are medical doctors—and women too of course—are addressed as such, but the others, Doctors of Literature and such, are not. I believe at the red brick universities, a Professor is addressed as "Professor" but not here in Oxford, where to do so is a social bêtise, as I discovered to my cost when I first entered university society. I was told that I was to be introduced to Professor X, and addressed him as such—looking over my head dreamily, the old buster said in a meditative voice, "When I was a young man the only persons addressed as Professor were professional conjurors"!

I indeed know only too well what Committees can be, for when I was in my prime I did a lot of back-stage Church work and sat on only too many of them. I still remember with a smile one after which a cynical fellow member remarked to me that he had never failed to find the petition "Prevent us Oh Lord in all our doings" granted at a Church Committee meeting!

I'm very sorry to hear that there is no prospect of your visiting this country, but I must admit I think you wise, if for weather reasons only. I bought a lightweight jacket the other day on the strength of the temperature being 83—five days later it was 54.

I'm glad I didn't notice until now your reference to Paisley, for if I had I should have become both unchristian and tedious.[135]

With all best wishes, yours sincerely, W. H. Lewis

---

135 Many resented Ian Paisley because the politician's uncompromising style was thought to estrange allies and prolong the brutality that was ravaging Northern Ireland.

## 33

2 August 1970

My dear Major Lewis,

It is nearly 3 weeks since your letter came. I did get the book off to you two weeks ago, and am very glad that you are happy to have it. I tried to find a decent map of New Britain to enclose, but did not succeed. As it goes by ship it will be some time in reaching you.

My dear Nance left us last Wednesday, with your address in her handbag, but no certainty of being able to visit you. I hope that she will; I will be glad to hear her impressions of you, and t'other way on! But Irene Markham, who might have been with her, has decided to come home much sooner; she is tired of travel and her money is running out. In a way I rejoice, as I hope she may be able to come back here. I could go for my leave with much more confidence if she were back there. I am very tired and possibly more stale than tired, and hope to get away in mid-October. But we must find another nurse first.

Yes, your Ireland has been very much in our news,

especially at the Battle of the Boyne celebrations.[136] I wonder if your "Irish" reaction to the T. V. scene with the widowed Protestant woman would have been as violent if that same woman had been a Roman Catholic? Is it the easily excited Irish nature that is roused, or the partisan spirit?

Next week, with luck, I shall be going to the Combined Churches' Medical Council in Goroka, which is 5000 ft above sea level, so we should be rather cool.[137] Already I have had letters from the Plymouth Brethren Secretary, a nun, and a conversation on the radio with a Presbyterian doctor, all saying how much they look forward to our meeting again. It would be wonderful if that brotherliness could somehow be born in the Irish heart.

I am horrified at the price of steak in England! We think ours is expensive at about 80 cents (8/-) a lb here. Living is rather frightening for people on stationary incomes, when the cost of living goes up and up.

Your preferences in music are interesting, but not in line with mine. Mine of course have been conditioned by my

---

136 The Battle of the Boyne, 1690, was a significant victory for the Protestant Prince William of Orange in the war for his defense of the English throne. The battle is celebrated as the turning point of the war and therefore the point at which a Protestant government was ensured in Ireland. It is commemorated on July 12 with widespread celebrations.

137 Goroka is the capital of the Eastern Highlands Province and home to approximately 19,000 people. Biggs would have traveled from Popondetta by plane, which would have taken about an hour and a half. While Goroka itself is quickly developing, the indigenous groups in the mountains around it are among the most isolated in the world.

education as yours will have been. Beethoven is my favourite; Bach in selected bits runs close. I do not like Ravel and not much of Debussy—in fact, there are few of what were the "moderns" 20 years ago that I do like! As for the more modern moderns, and the electronic sounds they produce—I can't bear them. But I was born conservative. I like piano and orchestral music, and vocal, better than any other. Nevertheless, I expect that we could both enjoy the same sort of concerts, if we had the opportunity.

Our Committees here are probably more productive than those you have served on, probably because we must be practical or perish. My helper in the spiritual life, F. Geoffrey, says that the Church must reconsider her role, get rid of her institutions, committees, organizations and what-not, and be more like a Flying Squad, ready to help where needed, but to let Governments and voluntary bodies carry the financial and organizing burden. That is largely what the Friars do. His word is "the Christian must be available"—and when one thinks it over, that is a mighty commitment. Fr. Geoff has just been elected Minister General of S. S. F., and so the Pacific will be losing him to the Northern Hemisphere, very largely.[138] We are very sad about that, though it is an excellent choice.

So you heard about the Sefoa motor boat. Fr. Denis predecessor's predecessor used to take me in that boat to Tufi when I was working down there; out of his fjord into the

---

138 The S. S. F. is the Society of St. Francis, an Anglican Franciscan Community. The S. S. F. is split into four orders, each of which is led by a Minister General.

open sea and round into the Tufi fjord. It is flat-bottomed, and came down with a mighty smack on each wave so that I would arrive with a violent headache! I think I would have preferred walking down one 400-foot slope, up on the other side of the fjord, and down yet again, but he loved helping me and that was that. Boats and engines have a short life in this country.

I have a little map of Oxford, mainly that area occupied by the Colleges, in a sort of Guide Book. Is Headington to the North, South, East, or West? From memory, on our very brief visit we approached Oxford from the east (from London) and went out westward to see Blenheim Castle, which I did not like a bit. Would we have gone through Headington? I suppose that the Quarry is no longer a Quarry?

I had rather an odd experience recently, at Matins. Some train of thought ran through my head, and it occurred to me that that was the way your brother would have thought out the same matter; then I had a feeling that he was there in the spirit. It was not a vivid, shattering experience, but just a pleasant, comforting one. I have occasionally had much the same feeling about my dead sister.[139] Perhaps some day we will know what it is all about. If you and I do not meet in this life, I hope that we shall in the next.

Are you being burdened with the American tourists again this summer? Probably it is an annual event! Our uninvited guests are usually Government officials and students.

All good wishes to you,

---

139 This sister is probably Lillian, who passed away in 1967.

# 34

13 August 1970

Dear Dr. Biggs,

Many thanks for yours of the 2nd, which seems to have got here rather quicker than is usual.

If your friend contacts me I need hardly say that it will be a great pleasure to meet her (but I do hope she doesn't think it one of the things she has got to do). I would of course prefer that it should be you, but that alas seems to be out of the sphere of practical politics. Mid-Oct. is still a long way off and I am concerned to hear that you are feeling the strain at Popondetta so badly. Anyway, I do hope that your visit to a hill station, even if it was duty not holiday, will have bucked you up a bit.

Poor Ulster, things are if anything rather worse than better, and the last outrage has worried even the English—15 lbs of gelignite[140] as a booby trap on the unlocked door of an abandoned car, which blew two policemen into small

---

140 Gelignite is an explosive made by dissolving gun cotton in wood pulp, potassium, or sodium nitrate. It is inexpensive and easily stored.

fragments—the cold-blooded wickedness of it![141] It might just as easily been a bunch of schoolchildren who decided to investigate that car. This more or less proves what I've long suspected, namely that the Irish Republican Army is taking a hand in the game; it has their smell about it, for a crueler set of blackguards never infested poor Ireland.[142] They are a banned organization in their own country. Then it is thought too that the Communists are fishing in troubled waters; it came out last week that someone is offering the Belfast rabble £2 a day to provoke street "incidents." The only solution I can see is to declare Martial Law and then arrest all trouble-makers and put them in concentration camps until the heat is off. But enough of our troubles.

Your Fr. Geoffrey sounds a man with interesting ideas, but how can one do without organizations? Any senior policeman will tell you that Flying Squads need a deal of organizing! One idea here is that the introduction of "pop" hymns, complete with a three piece "pop" band, brings people into Church. No doubt: and a strip tease act would fill it to capacity. But is this in any sense Christianity? Though mind you something of the sort can be both reverent and effective. I heard a TV church service the other night where the chil-dren's choir sang negro spirituals, both reverently and with

---

141  On August 11, 1970, two Royal Ulster Constabulary (RUC) officers were killed in this explosion.

142  The Irish Republican Army (IRA) refers to several forces that held a strong commitment to the idea that all of Ireland should be free and independent and that the use of violence was the best means to accomplish that goal.

obvious enthusiasm. Then there is the "Church Union" idea which is to my way of thinking a surrender of belief by both the contracting parties; and anyway, when we remember that the most regular churchgoers are the R. C.s, and that their hierarchy refuses even considering amalgamation, this seems no outlet.

We are about 3 miles from the city centre, and if you approached from London you must have run through Headington; the Quarry, as you have guessed, is no longer worked, but many of the old pits survive, and from them came the stone for several of the Oxford colleges. We are now a peaceful community, but our bad reputation survives—as late as World War I, policemen were not allowed into Quarry after dark except in couples!

Yes, the tourist season is in full swing, but by no means all Americans; last week I was in Oxford and saw two Swiss coaches, one Italian, and one Spanish, all within ten minutes. Poor things, how bored they looked as the guide hounded them into what was probably their tenth college!

As ever, Warren Lewis

## 35

6 September 1970

My dear Major Lewis

Your last letter with two photographs came in just seven days. Thank you for all three. At least it proves that England sometimes has weather suitable for open-necked shirts! That photo will keep company with the earlier one you sent, with a background of gorse. The cottage is charming, but lonely—maybe that is its attraction? It looks more lonely because of the lack of trees. I suppose it is peat country?

To return the compliment I had my photograph taken at the recent Conference. I asked our Publicity lass to take one as she was using her camera for press purposes. She has promised to send me a few prints if they are successful, so they must wait till the next letter. Nance has my own camera overseas. Actually, I do not like having my photo taken maybe through vanity; I don't take a particularly good one.

Nance arrives in England on the 8th, next Tuesday. Her tour trip to Oxford is on the 15th, having slept at Stratford and on route Windsor, so there will be little time, probably only an hour or so in the morning. It is World Christian Tours (Cooks) if you happen to see their coach about. However, if she is to visit you, it is pretty sure to be later on. I am sure she does not feel hounded into going to see you; if she does arrive, it will be because she wishes to go; but if she does not arrive, it is just as likely to be because she has no time. Betsy Ashton may be driving her.[143] Betsy is a nurse who has worked out here with me for odd periods.

The Conferences at Goroka were entirely different from each other but equally good. I had to stay one night on route at Ukarumpa, an actual missionary township, run by the S. I. L. (Summer Institute of Linguistics) who send out their people two by two to study some of the many languages here.[144] They do not preach or proselytize, but aim to translate the Bible and other books. The night's accommodation cost me $14.10, whereas to a non-missionary it would have cost $38. They are at 5000 feet also and the air was so wonderfully fresh and clear that it was sheer joy just to breathe it in—after our muggy lowlands.

The guest speaker at one Conference was a Nigerian Professor, very knowledgeable, very charming, very sensible,

---

143 Betsy Ashton, a nun, volunteered on the nursing staff from 1962-64, and again from 1977-78.

144 The Summer Institute of Linguistics (now known as SIL International) was founded by Wycliffe Bible Translators in 1934 for the purpose of studying languages, promoting literacy, and translating the Bible, especially into languages that are less well known. In 1979, SIL International was awarded a UNESCO Literacy Prize for its work in Papua New Guinea. The organization is currently active in more than 50 countries. It is headquartered in Dallas, Texas.

and a good Anglican. The Rector of Goroka told me that he had visited him to find out the times of services on the Sunday. His jet black skin looked odd against all the brown skins of the New Guinea folk.[145]

The Combined Churches Conference was good too; an excellent spirit amongst them and the retiring President nominated me to succeed him. I'm not much good at that sort of thing, but better at the donkey work of a secretary. However, the new Secretary is a very able nurse from the United States. Now this will make you raise your eyebrows: we are hoping at the next Conference to have a combined communion service. The United Church man said he would want it, but only if all partook; I thought that it would have great value, whether everyone partook or not; the man on the Committee seemed to think that her Bishop might give permission for his flock to receive the Sacrament. Our Bishop's comment on her Bishop was "Of course he is rather a rebel and is faraway from the Pope to disobey him at times! But the Archbishop of Moresby may be a harder nut to crack." We have a year to work on the possibilities. Our Bishop was invited to read the Gospel at the Mass of Consecration of the new Roman Cathedral in Moresby—and was glad to accept. But I do not think that union means the same thing as amalgamation, any more than marriage means the losing of one identity in the other. But in the one case as in the other, I quite agree that union probably means conflict of ideas and adjustment.

---

145 This conference was the Medical Society Symposium. The speaker was Professor Lucas from Nigeria, a delegate to the Australia New Zealand America Society (ANZAS) conference in Port Moresby.

At our purely Anglican Regional Conference just 20-odd miles away, we also were introduced to what one might call "pop" hymns; the Friars are encouraging the use of guitars in Church worship, as every Papuan adores guitar twanging, musical or not. Some of the indigenous Friars are writing hymns in the guitar style with their own modes of thought, and our Papuan Bishop is writing hymns using Papuan language, chants and concepts. We learned some of them and they obviously mean more to the native people than the Ancient & Modern product. If it will help them in worship we are bound to encourage it.

Perhaps I was too sweeping in saying that Fr. Geoff would do away with all organization; but he did mean that for "works of mercy"—hostels for students, relief of famine, Save the Children etc. we should work with the non-Church organizations rather than start our own.

Will you soon be going away for your autumn holiday? I think you said it was an annual event, like the Spring trip to Ireland. I hope, but with no certainty as yet, that I will get away from here about the 15th October, in time for the Hobart Spring. They have had a wicked winter, and a week ago were having serious floods in N. W. Tasmania.[146] Space is used!

All good wishes,

---

146 On the 24th of August, 1970, there was record flooding around the Mersey and Meander rivers. The damage was estimated to exceed 5 million dollars, and there was one fatality.

# 36

17 September 1970

*[The following note was handwritten at the top of the next letter]*
P.S. Sorry to cut you so short, but I'm off for a fortnight's holiday.

My dear Dr. Biggs,

These mails are something of a mystery, aren't they? Yours of the 6th arrived yesterday, 16th, twenty-four hours after your friend had passed through Oxford, if she adhered to timetable. And anyway even if she had been here on 15th and had rung up, there would have been no result, for we were all over the border in Gloucestershire visiting a friend. Just to complete the irritation, I should add that "a day out" is a thing which happens to us about four times a year! Well, there it is; but when next you write to or see her you might explain why she got no response to her phone call if she made one.

I'm glad to hear about the photo, for the only one I have of you, as I think you may remember, is taken from a periodical—and except those in the shiny society magazines, these are never very successful. I look forward to its arrival.

Your conferences must have been nearly as good as a holiday, climatically speaking anyway. No one knows what fresh air means who hasn't lived in a low-lying tropical country and then escaped for a brief spell to a hill station, do they? We too have been attending conferences—on TV on Sunday nights, but on the whole, very disappointing, everyone hedging and qualifying; the result was practically valueless. None of the speakers would face up to the straight question, "Do you believe in miracles or not?" Except of course the atheists, who at least talked sense from their own deplorable point of view, saying that this is typical of the stories which have in all early stages of history grown up around a famous man. The only sensible comment came from a Christian woman who said she disbelieved in every miracle capable of natural explanation, and in those such as the Resurrection where no natural explanation fitted the facts, she was a believer.

I've been in hospital with a bad leg, and thereby hangs a tale. Whenever I am in such places I somehow or other acquire a sort of most favoured nation status and this was no exception. When Night Sister had made her rounds, Staff Nurse, her assistant and myself used to assemble for a jolly little furtive coffee party in Nurse's office—she a militant "shinner" i.e., a Southern Irishwoman who advocates the use of the Republican Army to coerce Ulster into a united Ireland—her assistant, a Roman Catholic from Falls Road, Belfast, the bitterest fighting street in my unhappy town, and Myself, third generation "Protestant Ascendancy" also from Belfast. And we got together like a house on fire. They discovered that disemboweling R. C.'s formed no part of my religion, and I discovered that their shapely stockings concealed feet and not cloven hoofs. If only there could be a bit more "get together" how different Irish life might be. We all parted after our last meeting with genuine regret.

I really don't know what to say about the combined Communion service, for I'm not sure how much my dislike of the idea is doctrinal and how much mere conservatism. But it astonished me that an R. C. Bishop should even consider the idea; he <u>must</u> surely believe in Transubstantiation and even the extreme High churchman does not hold that view—much less the Methodists and the rest.

As ever, Warren Lewis

## 37

11 October 1970

My dear Major Lewis,

It is some time since your letter came; yours took just one week, as against mine taking 10 days. You were clearly not meant to meet my Nance, who, by the way, is now back in Australia and spending the day with friends in Perth who were on the staff at Gona for years, working with Nance.[147] She says she tried to ring you up while she was in Oxford, but it was the wrong Major Lewis! Fancy Oxford having two of you! She must have left your address behind, so could not be sure of having the right one. In any case, you would not have been there. I am sorry you did not meet each other, but it can't be helped.

I hope that you have had a happy fortnight's holiday. England will be ablaze with autumn, no doubt. I wonder if you have many trees near your own home, to enjoy the change of the seasons at close quarters?

---

147 Gona is a coastal village less than 10 miles (16 km) from Popondetta. It is the site of an additional Anglican mission.

If you have to go to Hospital, at least you make sure that you do it under the most pleasant circumstances possible. I absolutely agree that the cure of our prejudices is to get to know people and find out that they are not fire-eating dragons.

You said in one letter that when you were more mobile you used to go to Concerts; so it seems that your leg is the cause of your lack of mobility.

My photograph has not arrived yet; maybe because the lass who took it forgot, or has been too busy, or because it was a failure. I had to write to Susan this week about publicity work we want her to do, and I jogged her memory about the picture. But I sent her letter to Port Moresby and yesterday I heard her speaking on our radio sched in the Highlands, so goodness knows when she and the letter will meet up with each other.

Rev. Ian Paisley is visiting Australia, neatly timing his visit to coincide with that of the Pope. I expect he means mischief, but I hope that Irish Australians are not as inflammable as the home variety. An ecumenical service is being arranged during the Pope's visit, and many of us are very disappointed that the Archbishop of Sydney (Anglican) will not attend. I am sure our beloved Philip who has just resigned as Primate would have been there; and the new Primate cannot be elected until early in 1971.[148]

Had things gone well, I would have been going on leave this weekend; however, things are going far from well. I still hope to get home in about a month. By that time Irene

---

148 Sir Philip Nigel Warrington Strong (1899-1983). See footnote 2.

Markham will be here and is to take over some of my tasks; and Nance will be back at the end of the month to lend stability to the place. But staff problems seem to be pretty well insuperable at this juncture, not only in this Hospital, but elsewhere. The whole Medical work of the Diocese seems to be at the cross-roads. One job I have before I go home is to join in two deputations to the Department of Public Health about the future of nurse-training and the future of medical work in general. This is one of the penalties of living in a rapidly-developing country; everyone is in a hurry to make changes, and no one agrees on what is the most desirable type of change. And the poor old Missions are caught between the cogs.

Miracles! I wish someone could tell me what a miracle is. I know that your brother wrote a book about them, and I have it; and am ashamed to say I have never managed to read it.[149] Again it is a matter of waiting for an opportunity combined with an active enough brain. Some people would say that the rising of the sun every morning, and the birth of every baby, are miracles, and according to my way of thinking, they are; there may be a scientific explanation of <u>how</u> it happens, but that does not take away the wonder of it. Even when there is no natural explanation of some phenomenon, there may well be one in 100 years time; certainly things do happen that at this stage of our knowledge we cannot explain. What does it matter, anyway; they are all works of God.

---

149 In *Miracles: A Preliminary Study*, C. S. Lewis analyzes the modern rejection of the supernatural and offers a logical argument for the existence of a beneficent, interventionist creator.

A Dr. Robert Shackleton[150] of the Bodleian Library spoke on the radio recently on 17th century life, and I wondered if he was a one-talk (or wontok, as Pidgin puts it) of yours.[151] You should have much in common, even though his interests probably extended over a wider field than France.

O, to come back to the subject of miracles: someone once said that we do not believe in Our Lord as God <u>because</u> He performed them.

I expect that I shall be here to receive your next letter; if not, the girls here will forward it on. Mail! I received a letter from a Papuan last night that was written on August 13th. Apparently it has been tucked in an odd corner on our Mission boat and made numerous trips up and down the coast! I once received one by Post Office mail that took eleven months to come from Port Moresby to me; probably tucked at the back of some pigeon-hole or in a neglected mailbag.

With all good wishes, and keep in good health, yours sincerely

---

150 Robert Shackleton (1919–1986) was a historian, philologist, and librarian. He served as director of the Bodleian Library from 1966–1979. He was appointed a Commander of the Order of the British Empire (CBE) in 1986.

151 The Pidgin word "wontok" or "wantok" is common in Papua New Guinea. It means "tribe" or "clan," and it comes from the expression "one-talk," meaning those who speak the same language. Biggs is suggesting that since Robertson and Lewis share such a keen interest in the same subject, they may be friends and professional colleagues.

## 38

13 October 1970

Dear Dr. Biggs,

The very interesting book has arrived safely and I tender my warmest thanks for it. I've not finished it, but have got in deep enough to get a pretty clear idea of a fascinating aspect of the war quite unknown to most people in this country. More important, I've developed an admiration for the Papuan or at any rate for the best amongst them. I can now pose as an expert on Papua amongst my uninformed friends!

What a queer mixture the Japanese are—incredibly brutal, a keen sense of art and beauty etc. one doesn't know what to make of them. Will their rapidly being Americanized have a good or ill effect? Some manifestations of it disgust and sadden me. One of the most beautiful things I ever visited was the Buddhist Temple of Kamakura, the only non-Christian place where I ever experienced a feeling that here was an atmosphere of holiness and live devotion.[152] This was in the

---

152 Lewis visited The Great Buddha of Kamakura in Japan on March 4, 1930. He was greatly moved by the experience, and two months

1930s and today?—Strung along its face in neon lights is the legend "Drink, Dine, and Dance at the Kamakura"!

This trouble-ridden island is in even deeper water than usual at the moment. There is a general strike of refuse disposal men, including the staff of the sewage farms with the result that every day millions of gallons of polluted water is being rationed and of course all the streets are piled high with what would normally be the contents of our ash bins. But for once my sympathy is with the strikers, whose wage is I'm told under £12 a week, which for a family man caught in today's inflation, is pretty near the hardship line.[153] And side by side with them we have the men who can afford to do nothing, just because they have three or four children! Where or when—if ever—the wage spiral is going to be checked we none of us know. In this morning's paper I read that the wages of a foreman in our local car factory have just been raised to £2,300 a year. The cost will of course as usual be passed on to the consumer.

Well, I can but withdraw to my books, being too old to make any effort to protest against things as they are today.

---

later, he renewed his Christian faith. In a diary entry dated May 13, 1930, Lewis writes, "On Saturday last, 9th, I started to say my prayers again after having discontinued doing so for more years than I care to remember: this was no sudden impulse but the result of a conviction of the truth of Christianity which has been growing on me for a considerable time: a conviction … which rests on the inherent improbability of the whole of existence being fortuitous."

153 The 1970s in England were characterized by rising tension between unions and the government over efforts to manage inflation. Strikes became increasingly common until the winter of 1978-1979.

I'm at present reading Parson Woodforde's Diary.[154] He lived 1758-1802 and was a delightful man, pious and charitable. I mention it for one very odd entry; in 1765, being laid up, he has to get a neighbouring parson to "administer the Sacrament in my church on Good Friday". So apparently the custom of not Communicating on that day is comparatively modern. I had thought it was a very old tradition of the Church.[155]

The Conservative Party Conference has just ended in an orgy of mutual back slapping and a promise of reduced taxation, increased social benefits and various other blessings which obviously cannot be combined. Do the politicians overestimate the stupidity of the electorate? I feel that they do. But of course the public memory is very short.

The weather as usual is wildly erratic, and today the indoor temperature with all heat turned off is 59F. (I suppose I shall soon have to make an effort to understand Centigrade now that we are being decimalized.)

With all good wishes, yours most sincerely, Warren Lewis

---

154 Reverend James Woodforde's journal, *The Diary of a Country Parson*, is a reflection on his life as a rural English clergyman.

155 Refraining from communion on Good Friday is an ancient Christian tradition. In the early church, a fast would be kept from Good Friday until the Easter communion service, and receiving communion on Good Friday would have been regarded as breaking that fast.

## 39

26 October 1970

Dear Dr. Biggs,

Many thanks for yours of the 11th which reached me on the 20th, and this I hope will have a kinder fate than the one dated 13th of August to which you refer. Yes, miracles. Well, I don't know that I would go so far as to call the birth of a baby a miracle unless you call God's creation of man and all animate life a miracle. But having for His own inscrutable purposes created life, then birth is merely one functioning part of the machine. But obviously the Resurrection is a miracle because that is directly opposed to the normal working of the terrestrial machine. My own attitude is to be as sceptical as possible about miracles, unlike the Roman Catholic who sees and seeks miracles in everything. For instance, the "miraculous" draught of fishes may have been a purely natural event, and so may have been some of the miracles of healing; we just don't know enough about the diseases to form an opinion. But as you see, it all turns on your definition of a miracle.

I'm sorry not to have seen Nance, but not surprised that

she failed to get me on the phone. I've just looked at the directory and I see there are <u>sixty-one</u> of us in Oxford District, two of whom are Majors. I'm surprised that so many holders of a Welsh name should be settled in one city in the English Midlands.

In spite of the apparent difficulties I still hope for the photo.

Trust that mannerless oaf Paisley to thrust in where he is not wanted! I haven't heard though that there has been any disturbance out there. In Ulster things go from bad to worse. We had a harrowing TV documentary last night on the situation—interview with a Protestant lad of 17 who had been blinded for life by shotgun wounds—interview with an R. C. mother of a 15 year old boy, shot dead coming home from Mass by a sniper —interview with an R. C. man, dangerously wounded in the back, but recovering. "Did you tell the police? asked the interviewer. "Tell the <u>police</u>" replied the man with astonishment (a Protestant would have made the same reply). "But," continued the man with lively satisfaction "I know who did it, and his time is coming". Another man, Protestant this time, said he could not remember at what stage in childhood he was encouraged to attack "Papish" children if it was reasonably safe to do so (and of course the R. C. child is brought up on exactly the same lines). The most sensible Protestant comment was from a man who said "We don't hate the Papists; we hate their church". Many well-educated people have long believed that the Irish R. C. hierarchy is primarily a political, not a religious body; they certainly supported the 1916 Easter Rising in Dublin.[156] I'm exasperated by Folk over here who explain to me that all that is needed to end the Ulster trouble is to compel children of both creeds to attend schools together which shall be strictly non-denominational![157] Well, if this shows the average Englishman's grasp of the problem – ?

Thanks, I did have a wonderful fortnight in Suffolk and enjoyed its peace and quiet, and as usual I was uncannily lucky in my weather—one wet day out of fourteen! My leg is no better and no worse, and after all at my age, it would be stupid to expect that the whole machine was not running down. When I think of the things I <u>might</u> have!

Yours as ever, Warren Lewis

---

156 Irish Republicans mounted a rebellion for the independence of Ireland from the United Kingdom during Easter Week of 1916. It lasted for six days before the greater force of the British military ended it.

157 As of 2017, only an estimated 7% of children in Northern Ireland attend non-denominational schools that integrate Roman Catholic and Protestant students.

# 40

15 November 1970

My dear Major Lewis,

As you will see by the Airletter form, I am at home on leave, at last. The busyness of preparing for leave explains why I have been slow in answering your two letters. Irene Markham returned one Friday, Nance the next, and there was all the handing-over of jobs to be done. They both looked so well after their holiday, with the bloom of a temperate climate on their faces. In the tropics, as you no doubt have experienced yourself, one's skin gets a muddy, tired appearance. I have been at home for one week now, and the climate we have experienced has been everything from sub-tropical to almost arctic! They say that England is to have a very hard winter, and we are to have a good summer; I don't know how the experts know these things, but I hope they are wrong as regards England.

I spent three days in Port Moresby on my way South, seeing people in connection with our Combined Churches' Medical Council, and Public Health, and a long talk with the Bishop, seeing sick staff in Hospital, etc., etc. I was even called one night at 2 a.m. to the Bishop who got a violent pain; I got him to Hospital where they decided (mercifully) that conservative treatment was indicated, and let him go home the next evening. I had a few horrid moments on the way to his house, imagining that he might have a fatal coronary and wondering how the Diocese would tick over if he were not to survive.

I also saw Susan Young, and asked about the photograph she took. She was apologetic, and had quite forgotten it. She is to have the prints taken off and will send them to me here, so it should not be long. Poor Susan is "publicity officer" for the Anglicans, The Melanesian Council of Churches and an Oecumenical Communications Group, as well as earning money by freelance writing, so she can be forgiven for forgetting photos!

Thank you for the picture you sent of the ruins of the Suffolk Church. Ruins always make me think of the generations of the simple people who worshipped there through the centuries. I am glad you had your peaceful holiday.

Your rubbish disposal strike has found its way into our news on many occasions; it must have assumed frightening proportions, and I am glad to know that it is ended, with higher wages for the workers. It is a mercy that there were no epidemics caused by the rubbish. We heard that drinking water was sold at some fantastic price, even though the authorities assured the public that the ordinary supplies were not contaminated. There are always unscrupulous people to make money out of any situation. In any case, anyone can boil their water if in doubt.

Leave has started off quite gaily, though I could not stand the pace, either in energy or finance, for long. My sister and I went to a Symphony Concert on Tuesday, a staff dinner for her school staff on Friday, and the Australian Ballet last night. All were quite delightful in their own way, although I continue not to like up-to-date music. An Australian has written a series of pieces: SUN 1, 2, etc.[158] We heard SUN 4, and I could not like it. But the Concert ended with Beethoven's 5th Symphony, which was wonderfully done. I have also been hearing a bit of Beethoven's Chamber Music this week, which I have not been familiar with before, but you say that you like it best. I enjoyed it, but like the full orchestra better, maybe because I know it better.

My sister has given me my birthday-cum-Christmas present in advance, the full New English Bible, including Apocrypha. I have used the N. E. B. New Testament for some time, and am more than prepared to use modern translations rather than the authorized version. I love, and to some extent appreciate, the old version, but the modern ones light up the meaning so much, especially with the Epistles which are very obscure, I think you will agree. I hope to sit down and read some of the N. E. B. straight ahead as a book as well as the daily snippets.

The Pope's visit comes towards the end of this month, I think, and we have heard little of the Rev. Ian's plans.[159] There

---

158 Peter Sculthorpe wrote Sun Music IV in 1967 for the Sydney Symphony Orchestra under the patronage of Sir Bernard Heinze.

159 Pope Paul VI visited Sydney, Australia, from November 30 to

was some talk of not allowing him a visa to enter the country at that time; while that might be a good idea, he would not scruple to make political capital of it. We as a whole were disappointed because our Archbishop of Sydney announced that he would not attend the ecumenical service being arranged by the Roman Catholics at that time. Most Anglicans in Australia would be in favour of it, I should imagine. This week the Roman Catholic Church in Tasmania is joining the Tasmanian Council of Churches, which seems to be making history.[160] There is a big service in our Cathedral on Wednesday to welcome them in, attended by all the member Churches. I imagine our Dean has had a big hand in this, but altogether relations seem good. Maybe Australia is going too fast for the English people?

Am rather curious about your camera: do you take the coloured photographs from the negatives, or are they taken from colour slides? My camera (which I rarely use these days) takes colour slides, and to make photographs of them is quite an expensive business. I must take some this leave, and see if I can get something decent to send to you.

The family—brother and two sisters-in-law, are coming to dinner, so I must stop and be ready for them.[161]

---

December 3 as part of an international tour that took him to nine countries.

160 The Tasmanian Council of Churches was one of the first in the world to accept the Roman Catholic Church as a member of the ecumenical council.

161 Biggs' brother Oscar had died in 1968, so these dinner guests would be Reginald, along with his wife Edith, and Oscar's widow Ella.

With all good wishes, and look after your leg, if it is the sort that suffers in the cold weather!

Yours sincerely,

## 41

23 November 1970

Dear Dr. Biggs,

What a surprise to get a letter from you written in Tasmania! Perhaps the nicest thing about the tropics is getting out of them. It is nearly fifty years ago since I found myself steaming north from my first tropical station, Sierra Leone, but I can still remember vividly the first night I came out on deck after dinner and was at once driven below by the cold breeze—and next day the astonishing grey look of the sea. I can also remember the astonishingly fresh look of all the women when we landed at Plymouth. You seem to be having a very full time, but don't overdo it and get back to your jungle in need of a holiday to recuperate from your holiday.

Thinking people are getting really uneasy about these constant strikes, demonstrations etc. and the Press has begun to come out with idea which many of us have entertained for some time past—that they are deliberately planned by some as the first move in a worldwide conspiracy to overthrow democracy. Oddly enough Russia is not suspected of being the instigator. It seems to be some force which wants to substitute for the status quo, not Marxism but Anarchy. I find it all very frightening.

I don't take the photos which I send you from time to time; they are done by Mr. Miller, and what the process he employs is I don't know; but as you say, they are expensive. I hope you haven't put a busy woman like Miss Young to any trouble over hers.

So far our winter is mild, wet, and unhealthy—so much so that all last week I've been confined to the house with a very heavy cold, a thing which as you probably know, is even more depressing than a real illness. Nor has my morning been much cheered by a Tax demand for a large sum for the year 1963/4! Why should these publicans be allowed to re-cast your tax seven years after it was paid?

I was born conservative and hate all change, but obviously we cannot cling to the old Bible for the beauty of its diction. It isn't a literary treat to be savored in idle moment, but a guidebook to a rule of life. Even in a modern dress I find some of it very difficult to understand, and only a scholar can appreciate the meaning of large sections of the A. V. [authorized version]. Of the Epistles my brother used to say that he wished God, in entrusting Paul with His message, had also seen fit to give him the capacity of orderly arrangement of his ideas. Even James found him hard to understand, you may remember.[162]

---

162 2 Peter 3:16 says that Paul's letters "contain some things that are hard to understand, which ignorant and unstable people distort, as they do the other Scriptures, to their own destruction" (NIV).

I was much amused to hear that Fr. Browning is still grumbling about his boat. If you haven't already done so, tell him when next you see him how much I regret having so narrowly missed making myself known to him.

No, I wouldn't say that ecumenically Australia is moving too fast for us over here. Where there is controversy in England, it is over the question of actual fusions, such as that under discussion of amalgamating with the Methodists. Personally I'm against union—if they are right, why don't we join them, and vice versa? Cooperation is however quite another matter and I'm in favor of it.

As ever,
Warren Lewis

## 42

13 December 1970

My dear Major Lewis,

This letter brings you my Christmas greetings, and I hope it arrives in time. Our Post Office people are threatening a strike, go-slow or complete, to celebrate Christmas, and maybe your P. O. people are following the electricians. Is that strike affecting you, or only the London area? It must be very hard, especially at this time of year. The bad part of strikes seems to be that they divide the world into two groups, "our side" for whom we fight to the last ditch, and "the others" who are not worth considering. But surely the two groups fuse, when the strikers and their families suffer on the other side. I can imagine a striker's wife dying because the Hospital had no power and could not operate on her.

We are planning a family Christmas, and it seems to involve us in eating <u>two</u> Christmas dinners in one day. We go to a niece for midday dinner and on to a brother for some sort of meal at about 5:30, getting off to a Carol service at 7:30 in the Cathedral. Both hostesses will be offended if we don't do justice to what they offer, so we will have to study tactful ways of saying No. We will probably go to the Midnight Mass on the Eve. I wonder what you do, if anything special?

My sister Win and I are trying to make plans for the future. We should both like to resign from our work at the end of 1972, and go overseas in 1973 for about six months, if the value of the dollar permits. We are told that money loses value by 3% every year, so it will need careful budgeting. We have been studying ways to invest money so that it will bring in a lot of interest, and also continue to appreciate in value, and also be a safe investment—but one can't have it all ways. I have an insurance policy coming up this week, and am quite enjoying the job of planning what to do with it.

The more I see of aging, the more I think that actual years have little to do with it. I have just had a check-up and the doctor tells me that I am very fit at almost 61. My sister-in-law at about 66 is prematurely old; a man died in Hobart this week at 99, who at the age of 92 walked part of the way up our 4000 feet Mt. Wellington. The Pope at 73 did a very good job during his visit to us; he stood up to a terrific programme in great heat; I don't know if the visit got into your newspapers, but he made a great impact on everyone, not only his own flock, but all Church people and people of no Church at all. Thank goodness your Rev. Ian stayed away.

Your old station of Sierra Leone is changing as much as the rest of tropical Africa, I expect. What a stormy country it is. I suppose you have no hankerings to revisit it? Many of our budding politicians in New Guinea are being sent to African emerging nations to study methods of Government; I hope it is helping them to learn what not to do, as well as what is good to be done. A few Africans come our way, too; a man from Ghana was on some United Nations fact-finding tour; and we met a charming Nigerian Professor this year. They do not seem to suffer from the lassitude that our coastal Papuans have. People attribute it to climate plus sundry tropical chronic diseases, most malaria and hookworm; and I should think that they would be as rife in tropical Africa. I suppose you caught malaria in your day? We keep it at bay with regular anti-malarials, but in the days of your service you would have only quinine which was not as good as present day drugs. During the war in New Guinea, the appearance of malaria in the troops was regarded as a self-inflicted wound.[163]

Susan has forgotten my photos again, I think; maybe I can do something about a picture at home; however, I don't really like getting my picture taken.

Hobart is really a lovely City; the river is visible from so many hills and the mountain is close enough to really belong to the City. Its architecture was really good in the early days (1803 onwards) but now they are pulling down some of the handsome stone buildings to put up concrete and glass boxes many stories high, bother them. The public puts in protests and even carries the day sometimes. My brother built his house where no one could ever build out his view, and it is certainly a magnificent one; but the price he and his wife pay is having to climb a terrific number of steps of great steepness.

---

163 Malaria was so easy to prevent that if a soldier were to contract the disease, it was perceived as an attempt to avoid service in the military; therefore, it was labeled self-inflicted.

When they become too helpless to climb them, they will be in trouble.

I hope that you will have a very blessed Christmas, with or without the benefit of the traditional social accompaniments!

Yours very sincerely,

# 42

19 December 1970

Dear Dr. Biggs,

I'm afraid that even by Air Mail it is now useless to send you my best wishes for a happy Christmas; But I can—tho' not very hopefully—wish you a happy New Year.

Yes, the electric strike was a considerable nuisance all over the country, but we escaped better than many districts, and many neighbours, for we cook with gas. On the other hand our heating and of course light is electric. This of course meant long hours of darkness without even the dubious consolation of Television. I found it a humiliating self-revelation. One couldn't spend more than eight hours in bed, and the long empty hours have shown to me the poverty of my own mental resources. One would have expected it to be the ideal opportunity for a spiritual stocktaking, but I'm afraid I was conscious of little but cold and boredom. The serious aspect of the whole business was that so far as I could gather, it was not primarily an industrial dispute at all, but a political one—a challenge from the extremist elements of a very leftist Union as to whether the country was to be governed by the Trades Unions or by Parliament. Public sympathy is on the side of the strikers. This sometimes had a comic effect, as when infuriated farm people took to dumping loads of manure in the corridors of the Electricity offices! We are now girding up our loins to face the next strike, that of the railway men—which I think will certainly fail as today the railways cannot exercise any great pressure on the public.

Your Christmas programme sounds—organically—a tough one, specially as if I've got my geography right, it will be carried out under <u>midsummer</u> conditions! My own plans are simple and humble. I'll of course make my Christmas Communion and then will have a quiet cut at the turkey and plum pudding at home with perhaps one guest. My old grandfather, a man of very individual ideas, always refused to communicate on Christmas day. His theory was that it was a day of rejoicing on which he did not want to be reminded of a tragic death!

The solution of the old age and income problem seems to me to turn on whether you are going to leave dependents or not. I have those to whom I want to leave something, so I cannot take out a Life Policy which otherwise would be the ideal answer; for if I sold everything and bought one, I at 76 years and 6 months of age, would probably get 10-15% on my investment. By the way here is a bit of comfort for you that I extracted from a Chinese philosopher the other day—"the years between 60 and 70 are the happiest of one's life". I wouldn't go so far as that myself, but at least I'm free of the common delusion that youth is the happiest season. Did you ever meet any thoughtful person who wanted to be under 21 again? I'm sorry for the man who died at the age of 99; it's absurd to feel so I know, but wouldn't it irritate you to miss your century by such a narrow margin?

Certainly the Pope did an admirable tour, and I saw bits of it on TV, including a reconstruction of what was I suppose the white man's first landing in Australia. His whole tour was well covered by the Press over here. (I was glad to read yesterday that the wretched creature who tried to murder him is a mental case).[164]

Friend Ian [Paisley] is curiously quiet at the moment, hasn't seen in the news for weeks—perhaps because the Ulster government has begun to hand out exemplary sentences to the more effervescent of the troublemakers.

I don't think the Sierra Leone natives suffered from lassitude, but what we did notice was that they offered practically no resistance to disease when once it attacked them. They had no fight in them, and even when one got common or garden influenza, he would just turn his face to the wall and proceed to die. No, I escaped malaria, boils were my specialty. But I remember the precautionary routine very well. At sundown we would all be seated on the mess veranda and a waiter would appear with a huge tray laden with what appeared to be cocktails, but was in fact the regulation evening dose of quinine!

Hobart sounds delightful and I've always been sorry that

---

164 On November 17, 1970, Benjamin Mendoza attacked Pope Paul VI with a knife as the Pope arrived at the airport in Manila.

my wanderings never took me down into those parts. Now alas, the only island I'm like to visit in future is Ireland! With all good wishes, very sincerely, Warren Lewis

## 43

3 January 1971

My dear Major Lewis,

I must congratulate either you or the various postal services who see to our mails, for your letter arrived on Christmas Eve. Thank you for your good wishes. The poor postman was later and later each day, but still kept a cheerful face on it. His latest visit was after 5 p.m., where his normal time is about 10 a.m. I wonder if your postman, bakers etc. expect a Christmas gift from their customers? They do not in Tasmania, but I was shocked when I first went to Victoria to find that they almost demand a present! Which of course takes away any vestige of the ideal of giving presents.

I hope that you had a happy time; it sounds rather lonely, and it would be rather dreary to be alone on that day however much one might enjoy one's own company. I used to correspond with a dear old lady who, with her sisters, always invited some acquaintances from Old People's Homes for Christmas dinner. Australia tends to go to the other extreme, and has parties for a month beforehand for the so-called lonely, till they have a glut of it.

Do you not think that, had your electricity strike lasted longer, you would have adjusted yourself and found that you did have spiritual resources to cope with prolonged alone-ness? It is not easy to "switch off" one's normal life and suddenly become another person even though the inherent capacity is there. I remember hearing on the radio of a woman who was in solitary confinement for seven years under some Nazi order, who refused to let her mind go to seed. She recited poems, novels, etc., and she walked her cell counting the yards into miles and taking imaginary walking tours all over the Continent, reliving old experiences. She also made an abacus from bits of chewed bread and slivers of timber from her cell and did complicated arithmetic.[165] No story of her making a spiritual stocktaking!

My sister has been persuaded to try installing a T. V. set, although she has been strongly against it in the past. We have had one since before Christmas, and so saw the Queen's annual speech with many illustrations from her overseas tours. I expect that you saw it too. Such a possibility of sharing programmes does make mankind much more of a family. We also saw a very interesting interview by Malcolm Muggeridge of Mother Teresa of Calcutta, of whom I had read a bit. So a television has much to commend it, even though most of the

---

165 In 1949, Edith Bone was acting as a freelance correspondent in Budapest when she was accused of spying and arrested by the secret police. She was detained in solitary confinement for seven years. During that time, Bone developed a series of elaborate and ingenious ways to stay mentally occupied. She gave an account of her ordeal in *Seven Years Solitary*, published in 1957.

programmes have little value and can be great time-wasters. Last night we saw how the British system of justice works, mostly in the magistrates' Courts.

I wonder if your Grandfather would have approved of the various new liturgies which emphasise the continuing meaning of Christ's sacrifice on the Resurrection and Ascension? He would probably have objected quite violently and preferred to think of the Eucharist as merely a Memorial of His Passion. We reverted to the 1662 Liturgy this morning, whereas it is usually Series 2, and I begin to see that Series 2 has quite a lot to commend it. Win and I did not go to the Midnight Mass at Christmas after all; last year she had difficulty in getting a taxi to bring her home after it, and it was not very pleasant wandering through the streets in search of one. The buses stop before midnight. So we went at 8 a.m. after all. The flowers were glorious, and I thought that the women who arranged them (and it must have taken hours) had really given a fine Christmas present to God and to the congregation.

Our midsummer weather has been wintry! Christmas day itself was well nigh perfect, but since then we have had gales, floods, cold and rain, rain, rain. The poor yachtsmen in the Sydney Hobart race had a terrible voyage. We strolled round Constitution Dock where most of them are tied up, while waiting for a bus after Church this morning. I am not boat-minded, but they were a lovely sight.

Thank you for the assurance that this coming year be the best one. Browning of course would have taken and included the 70-80 decade in the 'best' to be.[166]

166 Biggs is alluding to poet Robert Browning's poem "Rabbi Ben Ezra."

It is eight weeks since I arrived home, and I am girding up my energies for the next two years. I plan to leave here in three weeks' time (24th or 25th) and make my way North, seeing friends in all the Capital cities. That is the advantage of traveling from the farthest North to the farthest South of the Continent: I can do it all on the same air-ticket and see my friends at little extra cost. All this will not be possible once I resign from the staff, of course. There is a wonderful family in New Guinea, and there are re-unions wherever I go. Even those who found the work and conditions too hard seem to have homesick feelings for New Guinea once they leave it.

I hope you are managing to keep warm: the Northern Hemisphere seems to be outdoing itself in giving the inhabitants cold weather. Let us hope that your gas workers don't follow the example of the electricity people and go on strike, or you would be without hot food!

Keep well: with all good wishes,

---

The first stanza begins, "Grow old along with me! / The best is yet to be, / the last of life, for which the first was made. / Our times are in His hand." As Biggs was typing this letter, the carbon paper slipped, and all that remains of the next paragraph of this letter are fragments, as follows: "my Mother saying that she was having the bes... probably in her seventies. She had had the st... work of bringing up a family of ten with not... the end she had moderate security and a daughter...; and her family all 'off her hands' but stil [sic] ... father wanted to live to be 100, which ... understand, as eyesight and hearing both steadily worsened. However, after Mother's death he lost the desire to see his century and died at 94."

# 44

14 January 1971

Dear Dr. Biggs,

Many thanks for yours of the 3rd.

Oh yes, we too suffer from those Christmas demands from all and sunder; this year the garbage men, who have only just ended a strike which put us all to much inconvenience and not a little health risk, had the impudence to turn up as usual with outstretched hand and "Merry Christmas". I am glad to say I haven't yet met anyone who gave them anything except some pungent winged words!

I don't really find my life a lonely one except in so far as all old age must be lonely owing to the steady disappearance of old friends and one's loss of touch with and sympathy towards contemporary ideas and morals. But if the present becomes less and less comprehensible, there is the compensating fact that the past becomes more vivid and more real every day— or at least this is what I find, but then I tend to live in the past deliberately, re-reading my old favourite books, ignoring the modern so far as is possible. Wisely or unwisely? I don't know.

But I do admire that prisoner in Nazi Germany enormously. It would be interesting to know what her age was.

I was interested in your reaction to TV which is broadly the same as my own; but one soon learns what are the worthwhile programmes and which should be avoided. If you have a programme called "Top of the Pops" it is worth looking at <u>once</u> just to see the depths of futility and vulgarity TV can descend to at its worst.[167] Not that I'm a highbrow, I enjoy a good thriller as much as the next man; it is in fact the pretentious pseudo-intellectual "problem play" that is my *bête noir*.[168] Muggeridge by the way has been taking the chair in a TV show on various aspects of religion, debated by opposing teams of half a dozen or so.[169] A good one last Sunday between Deists, i.e. Christians, Muhammadans, Jews, etc. and six "infidel dogs" to use Dr. Johnson's phrase. What surprised me was that no one put forward what to me is the strongest, non-revelation proof for Deism, namely that at no period as far back as we can reach do we find the atheist, who is a recent emergent; and is it credible that man, unassisted by inspiration, should have <u>invented</u> the fantastic theory of a Great Big Somebody up in the sky who had made man and controlled

---

167 *Top of the Pops* was a long-running BBC television show featuring live performances of the week's most popular musical hits.

168 A *bête noir* is a pet peeve, something strongly disliked, to be avoided at all costs.

169 Malcolm Muggeridge (1903-1990) was a controversial television personality who came to faith late in life. He published a treatise on faith in 1969 called *Jesus Rediscovered* and was received into the Catholic Church in 1982.

his destinies? I find this impossible to believe.

I was only thirteen when my grandfather died, so of course know nothing about his religious views except by hearsay, but I fancy they would have been permanently coloured by his own descent. His father was a Methodist Welsh farmer and preacher, sufficiently well known to be described as "The Grand Old Man of Methodism" in his full-column obituary in the local press. I haven't heard any of these new Liturgies myself; we are very old fashioned at Quarry.

I hope you enjoy your trip, and suppose you will be out of touch with civilization whilst on your trek.

With all best wishes, yours, Warren Lewis

# 45

1 March 1971

My dear Major Lewis,

As you see, I am back in Papua, and with my nose well down to the grindstone once more—but feeling well enough to cope with it. Your mail strike continues and continues, so that the only way one can communicate is by thought and prayer;[170] but Fr. and Mrs. [Ruth] Kelly are out here on a visit and will take mail back as they go. There are stories of substitute mail services within Britain. I shall tell them to send this to you if they can; if not, to destroy it. Fr. Kelly (very English in spite of his name) is the Organizing Secretary of the New Guinea Association in Britain. His wife is as glamorous, and very like, Princess Grace of the same name; so much so that we used to call her Grace Kelly behind her back.

The news from Ireland is again bad, after a lull. I expect that you are very concerned. Have you heard the Ian Paisley story of his death and request to enter the pearly gates? St.

---

170 This letter was sent with "St. Luke's Hospital" as the return address, in hopes that it would make its way to Lewis despite the mail strike.

Peter refused and sent him below. Soon St. Peter was besieged by a panic-stricken devil begging for political asylum!

For Lenten reading I am reading once more your brother's *Reflections on the Psalms*, which I chose since my daily reading is the Psalms in *The New English Bible*. My sister gave me a copy of the N. E. B. for my birthday. It is all very refreshing, when lit up by CSL's ideas.

You are in my thoughts, and there it must rest. This is so short that it will not matter if it does not reach you.

Yours, affectionately,

# 46

28 March 1971

My dear Major Lewis,

You have been much in my thoughts, as with other English friends who have been incommunicado for so long. What a shattering feeling it must be to be cut off from anyone out of visiting distance! However, one of our English staff, a rather homesick 20-year-old, had a letter over two months old from her Mother, who said that in her area a local postal service had been set up; I don't know its radius. Did you receive a letter from me posted by Father Kelly in England? I told him, if he was not able to post it quickly, to destroy it. I received an English calendar on Thursday, posted by surface mail last September. That took long enough and would not have been affected by the strike.

You will no doubt soon be going off on your Spring-time holiday. Our English girl says that Spring has come early in the North (I think Edinburgh) so I hope you also are getting good weather early.

At long last I have received the photographs from Susan

Young, and also some taken at home. None are particularly good, so I send two, hoping that the one may compensate for the deficiencies of the other. I despair of ever getting one that pleases me; I am getting it off before we hear confirmed the rumours that our postages are going up yet again. Ordinary letters are to cost 7 cents instead of 5 cents—nearly 50% rise. No doubt Britain will do likewise pretty soon, to pay for any rise in postal workers' wages. All workers of whatever category in Australia (except missionaries and pensioners!) got a rise of 6% as from January 1st, so all costs are spiraling.

I was sorry to hear that Major Chichester-Clarke had resigned; though I know little of it, he seemed to me to be the right man in the right place. The new man said he would be moderate, which may mean "weak." If so, heaven help poor Ireland![171]

Life here has been very busy since my return, with back work to catch up on, a Medical Committee with all its extra paper-work, a visit from the TB physician with all its paper-work, etc. etc. The TB physician for the first time was a Papuan, and he is very capable considering his lack of experience, and handles the patients very well. I am beginning to emerge from the heavy period and hope soon to be able to relax a bit. I also spoilt my reputation by getting a mild dose of malaria. I was one day late in taking my anti-malarial and that was enough to allow a break-through. I only lost one day from work.

---

171 James Chichester-Clarke (1923-2002) was the unionist Prime Minister of Northern Ireland from 1969 until 1971 when he resigned due to growing political dissent. He was succeeded by Brian Faulkner.

Our Bishop is in England just now, and returns after Easter. I miss him very badly, as some of the business that would normally go to him is coming to me, if in the medical sphere. On his behalf I had to refuse the return to the service of a nurse who had gone after proving most unsatisfactory. Her irate Papa has written me a "stinker" of a protest! I think I will put it gently on the Bishop's file to deal with when he returns. It would be nice if Bishop Hand could visit his old haunts (he is an Oxford man) and preach to you! If so, I hope you would introduce yourself to him! I believe that he is the man who first brought *Screwtape Letters* to my notice.[172]

All good wishes, and I hope you will have a happy Easter.

---

172 *The Screwtape Letters* by C. S. Lewis was first published in book form in February 1942.

**47**

1 April 1971

Dear Dr. Biggs,

Your letter of 1ˢᵗ March arrived yesterday and was a very pleasant surprise in a mail which on the whole was depressing. On seeing the stamped address of the sender I very nearly put it aside to be dealt with later on, thinking it must be an appeal. It was kind of you to think of this ingenious method of getting into touch with me once more. Yes, the substitute mail services worked remarkably well but of course could only be used domestically; here in Oxford our "pirate" post delivered by fast car anywhere within 150 miles or so in about 36/48 hours, charge 2/- per letter. Those of the banks and the big mail order houses were so efficient that I hear they talk of maintaining them as part of their normal business organization!

No, I hadn't heard the Paisley story, and I'm delighted with it. But alas, there is a sad and serious side to the whole business and I don't see any end to it. On the long term view of course, the obvious solution is to establish non-denominational schools and make attendance at them compulsory. But this is outside the range of practical politics; neither R. C.s nor Protestants would hear of such a thing for a moment. On the short term view old hands like myself who were in Belfast in 1922 cannot understand why they do not employ the methods which worked so well then, viz. internment of suspects without trial for an indefinite period.[173]

Oddly enough, I too have read *Reflections on the Psalms* as part of my hour a day during Lent and found the book helpful. And apropos of Lenten reading, do you know the answer to this puzzle which struck me for the first time only last week—how come that we have the story of the dream of Pilate's wife?[174] It doesn't seem the kind of thing she would have told anyone except Pilate, and if she did, her circle was presumably limited to Roman officials and their wives, who would have had no social contact with "natives"—certainly not natives of the social status of the synoptists.[175] A native housemaid perhaps, with a penchant for listening at keyholes? But this to me seems rather far-fetched.

---

173 The British government established The Civil Authorities (Special Powers) Act 1922. It allowed the government to "take all such steps and issue all such orders as may be necessary for preserving the peace and maintaining order," including permission for internment without trial, which was one of its most controversial provisions. The Civil Authorities Act was repealed in 1973.

174 According to Matthew 27:19, Pilate's wife sent a message to her husband, urging him not to prosecute Jesus because she had had a distressing dream.

175 A synoptist is a writer of one of the synoptic gospels: Matthew, Mark, or Luke.

How do you find yourself now that you are back in Papua? Did the harness gall a little on putting it on once more? I'm afraid it probably did. On the mundane level I expect traveling between Papua and civilization is much the same as doing so between Africa and England—homeward bound empty trunks and a satisfying bank statement, outward with plenty of new clothes and no money!

Yesterday was Budget Day and for a marvel there seems to be something for everyone in the measure. Better even than financial relief, we are promised a complete overhaul of the taxation system, which had become so complicated that even the weekly wage earner now has to employ a qualified Accountant to steer him through the jungle. What chiefly convinces me that it is a good Budget is the feebleness of the Opposition's objections to it.

Hoping to hear from you direct in the near future,

yours as ever, Warren Lewis

# 48

12 April 1971

Dr. Biggs,

Many thanks for yours of the 30th March and many more for the photos; it is in some sort like meeting you, or at any rate giving me a clearer idea of you. I cannot of course judge of its likeness, but note that you are not satisfied with it, which is a pity. I can return the compliment only with an indifferent snapshot. The sulky-looking layabout in the open-necked shirt is me; the other man is a dear American friend, Professor Kilby of Wheaton College who visits England most years and who always comes to Oxford.[176] We are taken on a jaunt to an interesting old chapel over in Buckinghamshire, which we went to after visiting the headquarters of the Hellfire Club

---

176 Clyde S. Kilby was a much-loved English professor at Wheaton College from 1931-1981. He studied the Inklings and became friends with several of them, including J. R. R. Tolkien and C. S. Lewis. He is the founder of Wheaton's Marion E. Wade Center, a collection of published and unpublished works by Tolkien, Lewis, Charles Williams, Owen Barfield, George Macdonald, G. K. Chesterton, and Dorothy L. Sayers.

of evil memory, about five miles from the chapel.[177]

No I haven't been away from here for Easter. One of the beauties of being a "has been" is that you need never take your holidays during the holiday seasons. Yesterday was Easter Sunday and I celebrated at our local church as usual—a most heartening sight, the church was more than three-quarters full, and a large congregation

Blanche Biggs. Photo courtesy of John Biggs. Used with permission. Note that the the actual photo does not accompany the letter.

was leaving after the first service when I arrived; true, a lot of them were folk one never sees except on this day, Christmas day, and Harvest thanksgiving, but a three times a year attendance is better than complete absence, isn't it? But DV I leave for Ireland on 8th June and will be away until 3rd July; but, *bien entendu*, I shall <u>not</u> be visiting my native Ulster.[178] Poor Ulster, how sad it all is and how impossible to make these English

---

177 Hellfire Clubs, exclusive gatherings of aristocrats with a penchant for debauchery, originated in the 18th Century. The most infamous was initiated by Sir Francis Dashwood, who excavated a series of caves above the village of West Wycombe in Buckinghamshire. The caves fell out of use, and after World War II, they were transformed into a tourist attraction.

178 "DV" is an abbreviation for *deo volente*, a Latin phrase meaning "God willing." *Bien entendu* is French for "of course."

people appreciate the situation! As for what you say about Chichester-Clarke's resignation, I don't know that it will make much difference. If the new man can get no more backing from Westminster than Clarke did, well then he will have to go too. In one way though I think he is a change for the better; C-C was one of the old landed gentry and spoke as such, whereas the new man is quite obviously a prosperous Belfast middle-class businessman, and as such may win the backing of a much larger electorate than Clarke. Judging from our TV news that scoundrel Paisley is trying to stir up further trouble with a series of provocative processions; why they don't put him in prison under their emergency powers I cannot imagine.

What bad luck that an old hand like yourself should be smitten by fever almost immediately on your return, but it is reassuring to learn that the attack was a mild one. I survived West Africa without contracting it, so have no personal experience, but those of us who were less lucky told me it left intense depression behind it. As if the place was not depressing enough for those in normal health! Yes, the backlog is the curse that hangs over every holiday and there are moments in which one asks oneself if holidays are worthwhile; and in your case the trouble is aggravated by the Bishop being out of the country. But cheer up, before you know it you will have overcome the problems that have accumulated during your leave—one does you know!

Don't talk to me about the cost of living—too depressing, isn't it?

With all my best wishes, as ever,
Warren Lewis

# 49

9 May 1971

My dear Major Lewis

You will think that I have deserted you, and so I have, to some extent. I have had the best of good intentions, and have put if off because Brother Ass has been misbehaving.[179] Two weeks ago had one of those depressing "drippy" colds that do not make one ill but make one miserable; that was followed by a viral neuralgia, which I have had before in mild form following other colds or viral infections; this one was quite crippling, the *tic douloureux* that I learned of as a student, but have seen only once.[180] Just a fierce stab of pain every few seconds somewhere on the right side of the head. It is better now, thank goodness, except for the depression that viruses

---

179 "Brother Ass" is the name used by St. Francis of Assisi to refer to his body.

180 *Tic douloureux*, or trigeminal neuralgia, is a syndrome affecting the trigeminal nerve, which controls motor function in the face. It is considered one of the most painful of conditions; the severe spasms can last anywhere from a few seconds to whole minutes.

so often leave behind. But if I talk of other things to you, perhaps the depression will go. We really are at the mercy of our physical selves. Anyway, I have a new insight into the so-called self-centredness of people who suffer a lot of pain; there is nothing else one can be but self-centred. And the rare people who hide their pain and take an interest in other people are heroes indeed.

Thank you for two letters and the photograph of yourself; you certainly are not "sulky"; whether you are a layabout I don't know, having never heard that delightful word. We say "rouseabout" which may mean the same thing—an odd-job man, preferably the one who does dirty odd jobs. But it gives me a different impression from the picture in the *Letters of CSL*.

We had a Retreat three weeks ago (yet another Sunday not devoted to letter-writing) which was very good indeed and gave us all a spiritual lift. I then started on your brother's *Miracles* which was very suited to Retreat reading, but has rather languished during the period of physical misery. In those times I go in for Mary Stewart and John Buchan—cloak-and-dagger stuff.[181]

Your holiday is coming soon and I hope that the Ireland that you see will restore your faith in her. Surely the whole island route as you did last year, and see your dream-cottage? Your warm period is our cool period, both welcome.

Our Bishop returns to the Territory tomorrow, I believe;

---

181 Mary Stewart was an English writer who initiated the genre of romantic mystery. John Buchan was a politician and author, best known for his adventure novels.

I must have a trip to Port Moresby soon, to see him, to chase the inefficient officials of the Public Health Department who are frightfully slow in sending us our grant-in-aid—and those cheques are the lifeblood of our work; and to see about our Combined Churches Medical Conference to come off in July. There is also a Seminar which I might be able to attend, on the changing face of the Territory. But my colleague has announced that he wants to fly to Australia at the same time! We have not worked out that little problem yet. Needless to say, my colleague has either private funds or relatives, I don't know which.

Papua seems to be exporting its young men to England; we have two local men there now, both of whom were my patients on frequent occasions as small schoolboys. One is doing a course at the University of Manchester under the wing of the New Guinea Education Department, and the other is a young priest who is doing some parish work in the Diocese of Norwich, followed by a term at Selly Oak. The Bishop is trying to enlarge the horizons of our young men in preparation for future responsibilities.

I must confess that I have never wondered about the source of the story of Pilate's wife's dream. Dorothy Sayers introduces quite feasible ideas about contact between the Procurator's household and the future early Christian church. It is possible that [*the copy is cut off here at the bottom of the page, then continues on the next*] at one time was the fate of the guards who ran away from the Tomb, if their silence was permanently bought by Caiaphas. One priest I asked thought that they were probably put to death for neglect of duty anyway. To return to Mrs. Pilate, there is no evidence, I imagine, to prove that she herself did not become a Christian and tell people herself in later years of her involvement.

The intricate workings of officialdom are quite entertaining, or would be if we were not in a hurry to know the answer. We have ever so many visits from Education officials, who are trying to decide whether they will take over this Hospital and make a school of it. Each group seems quite as important as the last, and each has a different idea of its possible usefulness, its value etc. and gives his opinion with conviction. They can't all win in the end! The Assistant Director said, "If I have my way it will never be a school." The technical expert advising the Director says he will do all in his power to have it made into a technical school. I asked if I was at liberty to tell my Director (Public Health) what was said and the reaction was immediate: "O dear NO". But, if the Director asks me, I should feel quite free to speak out; after all, I am not a servant of the Education Department.

This is the season for visitors, it seems; we have one sick priest here convalescing; one tired one (Bishop David's brother) having a week's rest; a young couple here for the weekend; as there was a party last night, we had a crowd here for dinner bathing and changing; on Tuesday it will be the Regional Secretary doing the Budget with me; and so on. I am sorry for the poor little housegirls who do the laundry! My paper has run out.

With all good wishes for now and for your holiday.

# 50

19 May 1971

Dear Dr. Biggs,

I thought I was about due for a letter from "Papooa" and was very glad to get one yesterday, yours of the 9ᵗʰ. But I am very sorry indeed to hear the reasons for your silence and pray that by now you are completely yourself again. I'd heard of course of the *Tic*, or rather read of it in old novels; but I'd always thought it was the sort of thing the early Victorian *malade imaginaire* suffered from—like "the vapours" or the "languors". Yes, the really Christian uncomplaining sufferer comes as near sainthood as anyone can do in an imperfect world. Apropos, do you even read the now forgotten and despised Charlotte M. Yonge, a great favourite of mine?[182] She nearly always has one daughter of a large family who is

---

182 Charlotte Mary Yonge (1823–1901) was an English novelist. She was astonishingly prolific, publishing more than 160 books. Her best-known works include *The Heir of Redclyffe, Heartsease,* and *The Daisy Chain.* Both C. S. Lewis and Warren Lewis were enthusiastic about her work.

compelled to spend her life on a sofa and is a good influence to the whole household—though probably all that was wrong with the unfortunate girl was a simple thing then undiagnosed—slipped disc.

A "layabout" differs from a "rouseabout" in that he does no work of any kind—lives on "unemployment benefit" i.e. on the taxpayer, supplementing his dole with a bit of the more cowardly type of theft—beating up an old woman who runs a little shop single-handed and stealing the contents of the till.

So you too are a Buchan fan? I go even further back than that, to Anthony Hope; when feeling really feeble I can always slip into Rudolph Rassendyl's gorgeous uniform and make love to the Queen of Ruritania![183]

I rather think you may have hit the nail on the head about Mrs. Pilate and the dream; quite possibly she was one of the *metuentes*, the so-to-put-it, associate members of the Synagogue, but not confirming to the Jewish food rules and so forth.[184] My brother once told me there was quite a large class of such people in the later Roman Empire. As for the fate of the guards on the tomb, I cannot check my memory, but aren't we <u>told</u> somewhere that they were executed? Anyway I've no doubt they were, for that was what happened to the warder who let St. Paul break prison.[185]

---

183 Rassendyl is a character in the 1894 novel *The Prisoner of Zenda* by Anthony Hope. It takes place in the fictional country of Ruritania.

184 *Metuentes* is the biblical term for God-fearing Gentiles. In the book of Acts, Paul refers to such people at Antioch, Thyatira, Thessalonica, and Athens.

185 In Acts chapter 12, we find the story of Peter's miraculous escape

Yes, I hope to start for Ireland on 8th next month and get home again on 4th July. A little early in the season you may think, but I want to get there and back before the annual strike of the car ferry crews—which I guess will be timed to disrupt the August holiday traffic and will be about the last few days of July. How sick we all are of these endless strikes! But the employers are at last beginning to hit back. Swan Hunter, the famous Tyneside shipbuilding yard, has one on at the moment and have told the men that if they don't come back on their contract terms they will shut the yard down permanently; and Heath is apparently going to try to instill some sense into the car workers by reducing the import tax on foreign cars—in other words "root hog, or die"![186]

So even in Papua one cannot, escape officialdom? But I feel sure that anything you are enduring is a fleabite compared with we sufferers in this country.

(Here I must break off to write to an American fundamentalist, who, good lady, sends me three foolscap sheets

---

from prison. Acts 12:18-19 reads: "In the morning, there was no small commotion among the soldiers as to what had become of Peter. After Herod had a thorough search made for him and did not find him, he cross-examined the guards and ordered that they be executed." Lewis may have confused this passage with Acts chapter 16, where Paul and Silas are imprisoned and released when the prison is shaken by an earthquake.

186 Sir Edward Heath (1916-2005), the Conservative Prime Minister of the United Kingdom during the Troubles, used this tactic of lowering import taxes on foreign cars to hold back inflationary wage claims in the automobile industry. "Root, hog, or die!" is an American expression meaning one must look out for oneself because no one else will. It dates from the early 1800s.

every ten days trying to convert me to her views!)[187]
As ever, Warren Lewis

---

187 So much paper would seem an extravagance to someone who had lived through wartime shortages.

# 51

30 May 1971

My dear Major Lewis,

As your departure for Ireland is imminent and as you do not have mail forwarded, I am hoping to get a short answer to you before you leave. As your birthday is also coming up, I can wish you a very happy one, somewhere in the wilds, I suppose. I hope that there will be someone to wish you a happy day; even one good wish makes all the difference between an occasion and a disappointment. Have a lovely holiday and I must not be jealous of you.

I agree with you that a firm stand is better with strikes, even if it hurts the employers' (and employees') pockets more; but it lays an even heavier obligation on the employers to be fair in its pay and conditions. Our Broken Hill Pty. Ltd, the huge steel works, have just put up the price of steel by 8%, having had to raise all wages by 6% in January, and the Trades Union bosses are accusing them of encouraging inflation.[188] I

188 The Broken Hill Proprietary Company Limited, founded in 1885, operated a silver and lead mine in New South Wales, Australia.

must confess that the announcement that all these big firms make millions of dollars profit annually make me wonder if they need to put up their prices quite so high.

No, the *tic douloureux* (which may be different from other tics) is far from being the vapours. However, I am quite better, and feel refreshed after 8 days in Port Moresby on business. I saw Public Health officials, the Hospital doctors about my patient, the Bishop about Mission affairs, and our Combined Churches' Executive had two meetings to plan our July Conference. I find that meeting people face to face is far more satisfactory than letters. Public Health were blaming us for not sending our claims in on time; we were blaming them for not paying the claims; and we found that our precious claims were sitting on someone's desk waiting for an official O. K. Now they are agreeing that we can bypass the intermediate official.

In Port Moresby I stayed with our Publicity Officer, a Fleet Street product, and quite an interesting one.[189] As usual, I inspected her bookshelves and she has many of the books that I either possess or would like to; including most of your brother's, most of Charles Williams', and Tolkien's—I forgot the title, but it is "The Ring-something."[190] I have read none of his, but hope to some day.

You had better retract that word "layabout", as I am sure

---

189 Fleet Street in London was the center of the British newspaper industry from around 1500 to the 1980s, attracting the most talented writers and publishers of the era.

190 Warren Lewis had heard J. R. R. Tolkien read *The Lord of the Rings* aloud at meetings of the Inklings, chapter by chapter as it was written.

the description does not suit you at all. It is a purely English term, I think.

I like Buchan, but am scarcely a fan; and I have read none of Anthony Hope.

Now I am going to surprise you, I hope. I am rather surprised myself. I am so tired of being bound to this place for lack of transport that I have bought myself a motorbike, Japanese make and specially designed for women with short legs.[191] It should arrive tomorrow having been registered, tested and an L-plate put on it.[192] Four of us here will be glad to use it on occasion and there has been some discussion about the ownership in just one person's name. Friends have given some money towards it, more than half. Now I must practice riding on our extensive grass (not good enough to be dignified by the name of lawns) and I know dozens of enthusiastic patients will shout after me and try to follow me. As my colleague goes on leave in October the bike will be invaluable for [*bottom of page—script cuts off here then resumes on the next page*]

We have Medical Committee this week, so I shall be well occupied for some weeks doing all the writing that follows a lot of decisions. We have a tight fit putting everyone up for the two nights. I will have two Bishops in my house, our neighbours will put up two Sisters, I hope, and the others may have to share bedrooms. All of them have to fly here except my colleague at Oro Bay, so it is expensive getting them all together. However the Bishops are nearby today as

191 This motorbike was most likely a Honda c70, or Cub.

192 An L-plate identifies drivers who hold a provisional license.

there was an Ordination at Gona and the one trip accomplishes both jobs. My job is so interesting, if only there were not so much of it!

I have not heard anyone or any book say that the guards at Christ's tomb were executed; though there may well be something written on the subject, and it seems the likely thing. It would be interesting if one could project oneself back into the past and know what really did happen!

I call three foolscap sheets every ten days pretty intensive proselytizing! How did you manage to stand up to that barrage? No doubt you get some amusement out of it. The Pentecostalist movement is gaining ground here and a sort of bastard version of it among the youth who reject all institutional religion, and do some rather weird things.

Have a happy holiday; all good wishes,

## 52

8 August 1971

My dear Major Lewis,

The letter postmarked 28th July arrived last Thursday, 5th August, telling me that you were sick. I am very grateful to Mr. Miller (your houseman?) for writing, though I suspected that something must be wrong and would have written before, if only other things had not kept interfering with my plans. I hope that you had Mr. Miller or someone to organize your return home. Traveling when one is ill is not much fun. I do hope you will soon be fit again, and that the sickness is one that leaves no aftermath. I wonder if you have been in Hospital, or being nursed at home?

News of Irish troubles keeps on appearing in the news, with just an item every few days. I hope that you were far from the trouble spots and able to enjoy some peace and refreshment; also to keep your Irish blood from boiling! We never hear of your Paisley these days.

Fr. Browning, whom you heard preach in Oxford last year, got a bad leg and has been quite ill with it; so he came here to be cared for and is in my house. I asked him this morning about the preaching and he said the only Church he preached in was Headington, which of course fits in. He has relatives living there. He is much better now and of course, fretting to go back to his hill-top; so he leaves us tomorrow. I doubt if he will be able to cope with all the hill climbing for much longer and have suggested to the Bishop that he should be moved to flatter country. Just now he is trying to adjust my precious motorbike, which refuses to start again if you stop it while hot. It starts perfectly when cold. I have decided to call her Jane.

My learning to ride her has been slow for a number of reasons; I did not get her for a long time because a friend was checking her over in his few spare moments; then I had a tumble off her, got a sprained wrist and a few bruises and still haven't got my confidence back too well; then the rain turned the place into a swamp (in the middle of the dry season!) the grass-cutter did not come so it was a long-haired swamp; then the rain stopped, and they resurfaced the road with skiddy gravel and bumpy stones! However, things are settling now.

It is the time of Conferences; we had a very useful inter-Mission one in July, and I thankfully handed over the Chairmanship to Sister Mary Lee, a nun who is also a very able doctor. I am on the Committee which is enlarged and autho-rized to have regular talks with the Department of Public Health on a proposed National Health Scheme. That was followed by a Medical Society Conference; and in two weeks we have our Synod. For that we planned to go to Dogura, our Cathedral "city"; but we have to fly and the airstrip will take only small planes. We could not get enough small ones and the cost was too great, so we are being allowed to use the Roman Catholic College near Port Moresby during its vacation. So you see, we are all very "chummy" with our fellow Missions. The R. C. Archbishop was to pay us a friendly visit this week, though we have none of his flock here as patients. However, he did not find the time.

You are now in the tourist season once more. Are you being swamped with visitors? I hope you are getting decent weather and get out into the garden to enjoy some sunshine. That is, if you have the sort of garden one enjoys sitting in?

While in Moresby I had the opportunity to hear Dr. Margaret Mead, who pioneered anthropology in this Territory in 1927, living for 6 months with a completely primitive tribe.[193] She has come back frequently since and watched the effect of our culture plus the presence of the Navy during the war, on her primitive villagers. At the lecture she spoke of the future, the using of the many N. G. cultures to fuse the tribes into one nation. She also dealt with her questioners and hecklers most ably. There is a young "Black Power move" growing here. She told one angry young man that if New Guinea killed all the foreigners to make a nation, New Guinea would find it was hating and killing itself, like Vietnam, Nigeria, Korea, etc. However, the angry young men are few and most relationships are very friendly.

You may have heard some echoes of the riots in Australia occasioned by the Springboks' Rugby team

---

193 Anthropologist Margaret Mead (1901-1978) worked extensively with South Pacific and Southeast Asian cultures.

touring Australia.[194] The protests were of course against Apartheid, but the protesters made themselves ridiculous, out of all proportion to the occasion. It would have been much better if the South Africans had not come. Now your English people are protesting against the closing of the shipbuilding yards which is a very serious matter.[195] Poor England. The Rolls Royce closure was bad enough.[196]

Our cost of living in Australia is jumping up month by month. My sister says that Tasmanian electricity charges have gone up by 17% in one jump. Certainly Tasmania electricity has in the past been the cheapest in Australia because of the huge reserves of hydro-electric power.

I hope you are soon well. With kindest regards

---

194 The riots referred to were in response to the South African Springboks' rugby team, which was racially selected to be all white. Protesters used this tour as a way to show their anger over the segregation happening in South Africa. Around 700 arrests were made during the team's six-week tour of Australia, and Queensland went so far as to declare a state of emergency.

195 A major shipbuilding consortium called Upper Clyde Shipbuilders (UCS) entered liquidation in 1971, causing severe financial hardship and a long, hard period of tensions and controversy.

196 In 1971, Rolls-Royce Limited experienced complete financial collapse as a result of mismanagement and the resulting cost overruns. The business was sold to a new government-owned company, and most of the assets were sold.

# 53

16 August 1971

Dear Dr. Biggs,

Many thanks for your very kind letter of the 8th, to which I'm afraid I will make a very short and dull reply. I'm just a week out of the hospital and am still a very wet rag—don't want to do anything, read, write, or even look out of the window— just like a cow in a field in fact, except that the cow has at least the diversion of eating. There was nothing really seriously the matter with me and I attribute my present condition more to the boredom and appalling food at the hospital than to any other cause. If my faithful Millers had not brought me down a picnic supper every evening to eat in the car I would have been ill in earnest I think.

The impression I formed was that the National Health Service spends 75% of its revenue on paying a huge clerical staff and the remainder on doctors and patients. As soon as I was fit to be tackled I was given a nine-quarto-page questionnaire to fill in. Believe me or not, the first two questions were "When did you get your first teeth?" and "When did you first walk?" Just the sort of information a man of 76 carries at his fingertips of course? I could have stood any of it except that they wouldn't leave me alone in my private room. Every morning there was a "discussion group" (i.e. a monologue by the biggest bore present) and every afternoon "occupational therapy"—for example one day we were assembled, each given a pot of paste, a sheet of rough paper and a pile of old illustrated magazines—and instructed to make a picture of our own composition with bits torn from the book and pasted on to the paper. I flatly declined to indulge in any such foolery and dropped into an uneasy slumber and finally was accepted as an oddity who must be allowed to go his own way. All that happened as I heard from my secret grapevine was that I was classed in the reports as "markedly un-cooperative".

Except for the actual dishing out of the food to the queue in workhouse fashion, there was, so far as I could see, no staff at all. The patients had to make their own beds, do out their bedrooms, keep the public rooms clean, and wash up after every meal. And here I must take off the hat to the patients—not one of them suggested that I should do any of these things and my offers to help were firmly refused.

It is significant of the age that the only question I was not asked in my questionnaire was what was my religion; one would have thought that even today this information would have been important in the case of an old man, even if only to find out which chaplain would have the job of burying him!

I'm ashamed of this miserable attempt to answer an

interesting letter, but the lethargy and selfishness of a sick man is still rather heavy upon me.

yours as ever, Warren Lewis

## 54

5 September 1971

My dear Major Lewis,

It was good of you to write to me while you were still in the doldrums from your stay in Hospital. I think some of the "wet-ragginess" must be due to the cause of your going into Hospital, though I am more than ready to believe that the "treatment" you received there added to it. Although I have read hard things criticizing the standard of care in American Hospitals, I had no idea that Britain had lost her Florence Nightingale standards also. Australia seems to be going the same way too. The trained nurses are far too busy being scientific or keeping records to see that the patient's bed is comfortable, his hot water bag hot, his drinks cold, etc. etc. As for the Questionnaires—I hope you felt well enough to give some really rude answers! I am sure that, had I been a fellow patient, I should have joined you in your rebellion and done what I pleased. Surely that sort of situation is one that justifies a strike.

Now that you are at home and under the care of your Mr.

Miller, I hope you are being fed well, and gaining interest and energy. Next time you are ill (I hope never) you will probably insist on staying at home. You ought to come to us for T. L. C. (do you know the nursing term?—Tender Loving Care) as our patients probably suffer from a surfeit of it. We have a young Friar in now, who is up to the sitting out of bed stage and he is in danger of being overwhelmed by too many interested visitors. There were ten in his room last night and I had to shoo eight of them out. They didn't like it, but the patient was grateful. I know that dreadful, imprisoned feeling of having unwanted visitors, and being unable to escape them or in politeness to ask them to go away. When I was sick years ago I used to sham sleep whenever I saw one well-meaning old man come.

Are you interested enough in life to read of the Irish troubles: they make sad-enough reading. Apparently your suggested tactics of interning the trouble-makers does not work this time.[197]

I still seem to be in a whirl of Conferences, goings away, etc. The Public Health Department considers that this Hospital is not justified as a TB-leprosy Hospital, and it is not, as many of our patients can go to their work or their villages as out-patients. They are seriously considering at this moment turning it into a training Hospital for Community Health Nurses, and I am not very clear what that means, except that such nurses would work in the bush and the main emphasis

---

197 On August 9, 1971, escalating violence in Northern Ireland prompted Prime Minister Faulkner to allow suspected terrorists to be detained indefinitely and without trial.

is on Prevention rather Cure of sickness. What it may mean for myself and our staff is not all clear at present; I hope to go to Port Moresby next week for a Committee meeting and at the same time talk to the powers-that-be about the future of our staff and patients. They want me to live at Popondetta, I believe, and I do not want to. I wondered, if I could become skillful enough on my motorbike, if I could live on here and "commute" when work in Popondetta needed me. But the roads can be pretty awful, either from floods, dust, or just bad quality.

Today I rode my Jane into Eroro for Church to talk to the local people about Synod, so the bike is being put to some useful service. It is years since I worshipped there, though it is only 3 miles away. In that time there have been new translations of the liturgy, hymns, etc., and I am amazed how much the language has changed in ten short years. I could not follow it without working it out with the English version. Synod was very good and inspiring, with a truly brotherly spirit. Even when difficult or controversial matters came up, there was a general smile as if even difficult matters could not disturb our friendship. Only once was that sense of unity broken and that was very ably handled. It was the first true Synod of this Diocese and as such was photographed, tape-recorded, filmed, etc. and it might even appear some day on your "telly". Who knows? We were the guests of the Roman Catholics and the Sisters were goodness itself. We used the Seminary Chapel and the staff and students even altered their times to fit in with ours. The R. C. Archbishop spoke hopefully.

My sister [Win] is at present Holidaying in Canberra with her best friend and they are planning a trip overseas in 1973, in the route of Marco Polo.[198] They say that, if one chooses one's time well, it is not unduly cold and there is not much camping to be done; so even oldies like us can do it in reasonable comfort. Thirty years ago I should have loved to do it the hard way, but not now; I have told them to make their plans and I will fit in if I can. If it comes off, we should reach England in about May 1973. These new plans about this Hospital may well have some bearing on when it will be right for me to resign from the Diocese. However, I am supposed to hand over to a Papuan for the supervision of the medical work, and there is no one with the education and sense of responsibility to do it as yet.

I think of you often and would like to be able to picture you as back to your usual state of health and interest in affairs.

With all good wishes and my prayers, your friend

---

198 Marco Polo (1245–1324) was an Italian merchant and explorer. He sailed across the Mediterranean to the Middle East, then traveled by caravan along the Silk Road to Beijing. After an extended stay in China, he sailed back by heading south along the coast of Asia, then circling up around India's west coast. From there, he went overland through western Asia to the Mediterranean Sea, and, finally, home.

55

14 September 1971

Dear Dr. Biggs,

Many thanks for your interesting letter of the 5th. The most interesting thing you have to tell me is that you may be in this country around May 1973, and if I am still alive then we must make plans for a meeting; wouldn't it be fun? So I shall live in hopes.

I thought of several sarcastic remarks I might have put on the questionnaire but didn't use any of them. They would have been wasted for when I handed in my form to one of the five girls in the office and told her I didn't guarantee the correctness of several of the answers, she gave me a dazzling smile and assured me that it didn't matter as "no one would ever read it"! About the same time the papers were carrying a report on one of our hospitals up North where the ratio of nurses to patients was 1/80, the ward beds were 18 inches apart, and the sanitary plumbing was out of order. Seems the National Health Service is due for a radical overhaul doesn't it?

Yes, indeed, I know the curse of the unwanted visitor. I was once in a hospital where, owing to a delirious patient who fought his sedative all night, I had—in the literal sense—no sleep whatever. Next afternoon, I was wakened by a visiting priest, to whom I grumpily explained my plight. "Ah well" he said, "You'll sleep all the better tonight for being wakened now"—and gave me fifty minutes of talk.

I'm not at all clear about your moves, reorganization, etc. You say you do not want to live in Popondetta, but I thought that was where you did live, it being your postal address. Anyway, I hope after the conference all will be settled to your satisfaction. I'm sure the Diocesan Synod will have been both interesting and profitable.

The Irish troubles? How could a Belfast man like myself fail to be both sad and anxious about the situation? Things go from bad to worse and last week there was furious rage when a little girl, aged I think 17 months, was shot dead in her pram; but I think it must have been an accident.[199] I'm not prepared to believe that even such filth as an IRA gunman could have done such a thing deliberately. The only hopeful sign of the week was a joint statement by the R. C. Bishops of Ulster condemning the IRA outrages, and this I presume was done on orders from their Archbishop in Dublin—if, as many believe, it is true that the President and the Dublin

---

199 On September 3, 1971, IRA snipers fired on British soldiers in Belfast. A bullet ricocheted and killed 17-month-old Angela Gallagher, who had been with her eight-year-old sister outside a sweet shop. The IRA later apologized for her death. Today, a plaque marks the site of the tragedy.

Parliament are mere "front men" for the R. C. Church. I'm surprised that the Govt. has not taken the step of putting the whole of Ulster under Martial Law—which means handing over the situation to the General Commanding over there who would have powers to make his own regulations and to try all offenders by Court Martial. But perhaps the idea has been mooted and turned down for some reason or other. It is all a long cry from the very happy church relations which seem to prevail in Papua.

Our "no summer" thank goodness is now definitely at an end and we have entered on a really lovely autumn which I hope is going to last, for at the end of the month we are slipping over to Ireland for a week to complete my cure.

As ever, Warren Lewis

# 56

24 October 1971

My dear Major Lewis,

I have not written for a long time, but it is not for lack of wanting to; life seems to be a series of extra demands, and my precious Sunday off is one of the first casualties. Last Sunday I did not even get my regular letter to my sister in Hobart, which is always No. 1 priority. We celebrated St. Luke's Day a day early, and it was really a lovely day, if exhausting. The Papuan Bishop arrived at 6.15 a.m. to take a Confirmation of two of our patients, then the St. Luke's celebration with the two newly confirmed taking their first Communion, then lots of extra people for breakfast, more for lunch, and still more for afternoon tea. Football, basketball, and lots of traditional dancing. The village people co-operated very well. Then, after getting off to sleep at 10 p.m. I was wakened at 2 with some of our dear patients singing and playing guitars with all their might in a nearby garden house. I ploughed my way with a hurricane lantern through tall grass and overgrown gardens and mud in the direction of the sound, berated them into silence, and then came back to bed to lie awake for more hours. The only consolation was that there was not a moon to entice them to keep on with their celebrations.

I do hope that you are quite fit again, and that your trip to Ireland polished you into a state of well-being. A week does not seem very long for that process. I wonder if you saw direct evidence of all the political troubles. It comes into our news fairly often and seems to get more bitter.

We have an English lass as Secretary, who is far from being the efficient person the word Secretary summons up; but she is very nice and very gifted in other ways. She came to my house this morning and read me a "poem" she has written which I take as a great compliment. The poem she read is a prayer in the form of a psalm, but very long, and shows great insight into spiritual reality. She says she does not write these things, but they come to her and she is compelled to write them as they come into her mind; in that way she feels they are a gift which she should pass on when the time seems ripe. I asked her about publication and she thinks that will come, but she will act only when action seems indicated. I wonder if you know of a Publisher who deals with that type of publication? It might be that the knowledge might be useful for her some day. Her only attempt to date has been to offer them for an anthology; they were accepted but she did not go on with it.

I do not explain my whereabouts to you very lucidly, do I? We live 23 miles from Popondetta, but that is our nearest Post Office. We have here only a few small villages, and acres of land lying idle. Eroro Mission is 3 miles further on <u>away</u>

from Popondetta, and St. Margaret's Hospital 4 miles further on at Oro Bay. The Bay promises to be a big centre some day, and they are beginning now by building an overseas wharf there, as it is the best harbour for a couple of hundred miles. It was a big Port during the war. After more conferring with the Public Health Department, it now looks as if our Hospital will continue here next year at a much reduced scale of activity, and all patients who can possibly be treated elsewhere as out-patients will be sent there. Then the Department wants me to supervise all the search for, diagnosis of, treatment and aftercare of all TB & Leprosy patients in the District.[200] They have even suggested that I might join the Public Service temporarily and be acting District Health Officer for a couple of months, living in Popondetta and combining the two jobs. The present D. H. O., a Papuan, is resigning in December to stand for the House of Assembly. If he is elected, they will need a permanent D. H. O. in his place; if he is not, I expect he will rejoin the Public Service and go back to his old job. They want me to fill the gap for the couple of months. It would have advantages, both for my work proper, since I could do the same lot of traveling to fulfill the two functions, and the salary could be higher, which would mean more money for the Mission coffers, which badly need it. The Mission takes all money paid to staff in recognition of their medical work, and we are all paid by the Mission at an equal rate, no matter what subsidy we earn. This Hospital receives much higher subsidies than general medical work does, and so it has meant

---

200 The areas that Biggs calls "districts" became provinces at Papua's independence in 1975.

a great amount of help for the rest of the medical work done by the Mission.

My beloved Nance Elliot retires in a month; she has been living in this Hospital although she has not been nursing, but doing the Diocesan sewing, cassocks, vestments, altar linen etc. etc. I will miss her dreadfully, but it is time she did retire and make a new life in Australia while she still is able to adapt to it. She and I are the "oldies" in this establishment, and one becomes aware of the generation gap. I wonder if your friend the Professor [Clyde S. Kilby] came to visit you this Summer? If so, his visit would probably have coincided with your period of illness. You probably missed out on the tourist season which seems to beset you each year. I put the photo of you and your Professor friend in my prayer book as a marker, so am often reminded of you. However, the photograph has been exposed to light more than is good for it, so it looks a bit faded. Talking of prayers, I find I need written prayers to help me, and they start me off, so to speak, and then I can go on to more personal ones. I am afraid meditation and contemplation in the sense of the Church fathers are both beyond me.

1973 seems to belong to another world, but no doubt it will come fast enough. I wonder if it will come and we really shall meet each other? I have two or three mental pictures of you, but nothing clear in my mind. Really, people who correspond know very little of each other's ordinary, everyday life. My sister's friend's present plan is to fly to England in late July 1973, and Win may well do the same, with her. I might (if I can still afford it) go earlier by the Marco Polo route and meet them when they arrive in July. But politics, wars and inflation might all decide otherwise.

Are you in favor of joining the Common Market? Our latest news says that a Gallup Poll puts 51% of British people as against it. Australia is not at all happy about seeing Britain join; it spells ruin to our primary producers, if they are not already ruined.

With all good wishes,

## 57

1 November 1971

Dear Dr. Biggs,

How nice to hear from you again, and eight days from Papua to my desk strikes me as pretty good going!

Yes, your celebrations sound to me very exhausting indeed, and not at all the way I'd like to spend a day in the tropics, but I'm sure there was a great sense of time well spent at the end of it. I'm no stranger to the nuisance of music, maddening in a tropic night; I remember to this day the celebration of Ramadan in West Africa when the tom-toms beat from sunset to sunrise.

Thanks for your enquiries about my health and I'm glad to say that I am myself again except that I seem to tire more easily than I used to do. But this is what one must expect as old age creeps on—with a prayer of thanks that things are no worse. The sad part of the Irish scene is that the troubles are peculiar to Ulster; in the North West and West where we go there is no trace of hostility, racial or religious—and in both places the hotel proprietors are Protestants and in one the population is divided religiously almost 50/50, all living on the best of terms together. But then they haven't got the curse of history behind them as we have in the North where *entre nous*, we Protestants were planted there by Queen Lizzie the First in order to dispossess the native Catholics, which we did.[201] You may say all this happened four hundred years ago, but unfortunately we have very long memories and the feud continues from generation to generation. We must ask God to solve the problem since it seems to be quite beyond the wit of man to solve it.

I don't know enough about your local conditions and present work to give any opinion about the changes which you foresee in the near future; but I am surprised that for you TB is still a problem, for as you know, over here it has virtually ceased to exist—though when I was a child it was still the nightmare of every mother—"The Great White Scourge" it was called.[202]

Yes, Professor Kilby is over here now and I'm expecting him in Oxford next week. He has been "doing" the Lakes, Wordsworth, Coleridge, Southey, old Uncle Tom Cobley and all[203]—presumably for the benefit of his American pupils.[204]

---

201 *Entre nous* is French for "between us."

202 Tuberculosis continues to be a serious threat in Papua New Guinea. Approximately 30,000 people per year are newly infected.

203 Tom Cobley is a character in an old Devon folk song called "Widecombe Fair." Its chorus ends with a very long list of people's names; the phrase "and Uncle Tom Cobley and all" is used to mean "and so on," often with a sense of exasperation or irritation.

204 Clyde S. Kilby took a small group of nine students with him on this trip to England.

Personally I've never been able to get any kick out of looking at the house in which a famous man lived, and have never bothered to visit the Marlborough place, though it is so to speak on my own back door![205]

Well, we've joined the Common Market and <u>still</u> haven't been told how it is to benefit us; all we know is that we've alienated Australia and New Zealand, endangered our fishing industry, and are about to raise our cost of living by 10%— not a very bright programme, is it?[206]

Personally I don't use any written Prayers except of course the Lord's and the morning and evening Collects, and then come my own blundering extempore efforts; but however approached, prayer is never easy, is it?[207]

Hoping to be still alive in 1973,
yours as ever, Warren Lewis

---

205 Lewis is referring to Blenheim Palace, one of the largest homes in England. Built in the early 1700s, the palace is the principal residence of the dukes of Marlborough. It is located about 10 miles from Lewis's home.

206 The Common Market was also known as the European Economic Community (ECC). The United Kingdom did not officially join until January of 1973. It has since left.

207 Both Lewis brothers would have used the written prayers, or collects, from *The Book of Common Prayer.*

# 58

5 December 1971

My dear Major Lewis,

Your letter of November 1st reached me on the 9th, so the time taken each way is roughly equal. Yet a package posted to me from Melbourne by surface mail on October 5th reached me on November 27th. The actual mailing time would not be more than 12 days. I have been, as usual, kept from personal affairs by other demands and so have not answered quickly. I also find that by the time the evening meal is over I just have no energy for anything demanding concentration, and so less is done in every 24 hours.

I hope that your well-being continues; after all, you are only in your seventies. We hear so often of lively, energetic people in their 80s and 90s. One man of 91 has just ridden a penny-farthing bicycle hundreds of miles around Australia.[208]

---

208 Biggs may be thinking of Dennis Wickham, who left London on March 30, 1970 and rode his penny-farthing bicycle 15,000 miles. He arrived in Brisbane, Australia, in November 1971. He was 32. The earliest form of the bicycle, the penny-farthing, featured a large front

And an old lady was interviewed and reported in the paper on her 106th birthday. Not having scores of descendants, I hope and pray that I shan't live to that kind of age.

No doubt your Professor Kilby finds that visiting the haunts of the Lake poets gives him some insight into their work and helps in his teaching. I am like him; I enjoy seeing the homes of famous peoples and trying to imagine them living there. I believe I have a picture of the school Wordsworth attended and saw his old home, and the Church where he worshipped. Maybe his idea of worship was not our idea! However, my sister and I also "did" Marlborough Palace and I did not like it a bit. I found it a forbidding place, and the gardens were not my idea of what a garden should be, and what so many English gardens really are. I remember that the few parks I saw in Italy depressed me in much the same way.

A couple of weeks ago I posted to you a trifle (we in Papua call it a "something-nothing") which cannot be called a Christmas present as it will arrive long after.[209] However, it is a model canoe, and a faithful copy of the canoes used in these waters, even though the lad who made it is an inland dweller. I hope that you will not have any trouble with Customs. England seems to be less fussy over Customs than Australia.

This is a developing country, and in many parts a primitive one, so TB is still with us. In many parts it is at least under control. It is interesting that in the squatter settlements in the Towns where conditions are slums of the worst order,

---

wheel and a much smaller back wheel.

209  In New Guinean Tok Pisin, Biggs' synonym for "trifle" would be spelled *samting nating*."

tuberculosis is on the increase, and even in people who have been fully treated in the past in their rural setting. Our TB specialist says that, even if one does nothing to combat the disease as such, but improves social conditions, the disease declines. We admit occasional new cases, most of them advanced, and try to follow up with their families; but it is very hard to get hold of them or persuade them to keep on with their treatment. By law they can be made to come to Hospital, but our police are not very co-operative. Leprosy, by the way, is definitely increasing, and it is my job to go looking for cases. The thinking among the specialists now is that a case of lepromatous leprosy, the more infectious kind, may need treatment for the rest of his life. It takes a lot of supervision and encouragement to keep that going!

My motorbike is useful in a limited way; the limitations come from the state of the roads. Three weeks ago I went to Popondetta by utility and the road was so good that I decided that I would ride the motorbike when I went off to Diocesan Council. By the time the Council was due two weeks later, I would not have risked the bike or my neck on the road! Great trucks carry 6 yards of gravel and earth all day every day and spoil the road as it is graded; but when the road and bridges are all complete we should have a good road. I ride the bike to local affairs and even take myself to Oro Bay for a swim occasionally.

My dear Nance Elliot has resigned and gone; that is the lass who was to have visited you last year. She flew off to Lae last Sunday, and we spent the weekend together near Popondetta; I saw her off in the little Aero Club plane, then came back to work. She is seeing a little of the Highlands—and she will today be enjoying a cool day at 5000-odd feet—then goes to Australia to make a new life. At present she does not know where she will live or what she will do. We have worked together for 24 years, and I dread the months ahead without her. She is to have a holiday with my sister in Hobart during that sister's Christmas holiday.

We heard on the news yesterday that the British Government is planning to double the Queen's "pocket-money" to a mere $2 million. That is an indication of how the British cost of living is going up. In Australia the Prime Minister's salary is to go up by about $7000, and all the members of Parliament in proportion, but the most they can afford the pensioners is a rise of 50 cents per week! I find money very confusing, and no doubt you do too. The more money one has, the less money one has. But life goes on much the same and we still have three meals a day and a house to live in. No doubt Britain will feel the benefit of the European Common Market in due course; and when the world money system settles down to something like normality we may know better how we stand.

A jeep has just driven in, no doubt depositing a visitor for lunch, or maybe a patient to be seen. I had better stop and go and see what it is all about.

This letter brings you wishes for a very happy Christmas, with food for the spirit and also nice things to eat. Do you have your Christmas alone, or do you have friends to share it with?

## 59

8 December 1971

Dear Dr. Biggs,

Many thanks for your interesting letter of the 5th; and as I much doubt this reaching you by the 25th. I'll wish you a happy New Year and thanks too for asking after my health which thank God continues to be good, barring the minor disadvantages of age; but I fear I shall never ride a bicycle round Great Britain, much less round Australia! You say nothing about your own health which leads me to hope that all is well.

Yes, the Queen is to get a raise, but poor dear, none of it will be pocket money; the whole lot will be absorbed in wages, maintenance etc. of her various residences. Even then the Leftists in Parliament will hardly raise a snarl I imagine—they having just voted themselves a 34% increase whilst urging the working man to "show restraint" and limit his demands to around 9-10% increase. The impudence of it!

I'm sorry (for your sake) that Miss Elliot has retired but from all you tell me of your work she has earned her rest—and no doubt will soon be finding some outlet for her energies in Australia. The whole of this question of leisure is a headache to the more thoughtful sociologists over here; how are we to train our people for leisure at an early age? As mechanisation, computerization and so on, take over, there will be fewer and fewer jobs and ultimately more than half the population will be "unemployed" for life as soon as they leave school. What on earth are we to do with them? However, thank goodness, you and I don't have to worry about a problem which won't I suppose become acute for another 40 or 50 years.

This miserable, wicked civil war in Ireland continues to haunt us all, and has now ceased, even ostensibly, to be a religious struggle. In the recent cruel outrage, when fifteen people, including women and children, were killed in a public house, most of them must have been Catholics; the situation of the pub establishes that; and the last three members of the Ulster defense regiment murdered were all three Catholics.[210] What a pity no one has a bomb to spare for Senator Kennedy—d—- his impudence! What business is it of his how Westminster or Stormont deal with our domestic problems?[211]

One domestic by-product of the business is that my

---

210 Lewis refers to the tragedy that occurred on December 4, 1971, when an Ulster bomb killed fifteen Catholic civilians at McGurk's Bar in Belfast, Northern Ireland. It was the deadliest attack that Belfast saw during the Troubles; in total, the thirty-year conflict led to over 2,000 civilian deaths in Northern Ireland.

211 In October 1971, Senator Ted Kennedy gave a series of speeches endorsing a united Ireland.

housekeeper, Mrs. Miller, flatly refuses to visit Ireland in 1972 so I've got to consider alternatives. Probably Cornwall I think, which none of us has ever visited—and having seen John o' Groats, I really ought to see Land's End![212]

I'm rather surprised to learn that there are any roads in Papua on which at any time one can ride a motorbike; I'd sooner have a swim with you at Oro Bay than a ride on your carrier. I'd have thought there would be too many sharks in your waters to allow safe bathing. But perhaps as we had at Singapore, you have "pagars"—a strong wire mesh fence carried out about six feet into the sea—six feet depth I mean.

So far we are having a very mild winter, but then the worst of our weather usually comes in the New Year, so we won't shout until we are out of the wood!

With all best wishes, yours as ever, Warren Lewis

---

212 John o' Groats is a small village in the northeast of Scotland; Land's End is in Cornwall in the southwest corner of England. To travel from John o' Groats to Land's End is to journey the entire length of the island of Great Britain.

# 60

16 January 1972

My dear Major Lewis,

I feel very much at home with the Lewis family just now. The reason? The girls here gave me Letters to an American Lady edited by your friend Professor Kilby as a birthday present.[213] I read it in bits in bed by torchlight after the generator has shut down for the night. It amazes me, as it clearly amazed the Editor, that your brother could drive himself on to write letters when it was a job he did not like, and when he was

---

213 *Letters to an American Lady* (1971) contains 135 letters, all of them written by C. S. Lewis to Mary Willis Shelburne, a widow from Washington, D. C. The letters begin in 1950, and end when C. S. Lewis died in 1963. In these letters, there are only two references to Warren being away. Biggs is likely responding to a letter from C. S. Lewis written February 17, 1957: "If I write very shortly it is not because I am reticent but because I am tired and busy. My brother is also ill and causes a good deal of anxiety, and of course I lose his secretarial help; so that I have not only much to bear but also much to <u>do</u>. I can't type; you can hardly conceive what hundreds of hours a year I spend coaxing a rheumatic wrist to drive this pen across paper" (*Letters to an American Lady*, 65-66).

in pain and "cab-horse tired" (I think that is a wonderfully descriptive expression). To compare it with my own smaller efforts, I know the fatigue, but I like writing letters as well as receiving them—do you? It is only when they are too frequent and too demanding and must be answered as quickly as possible, that I find it a burden. Nowadays I have the services of a shorthand typist for one day a week and so get my Medical Secretariat letters reasonably up-to-date with her help. My busy-ness explains why I have not written to you more promptly, although each Sunday I planned to write. Visitors etc. on Sunday are frequent and not very welcome as it is my only free day. Your letter to me came on Dec. 23rd, which was quite quick.

One thing that struck me in the new book (I am only half-way through as yet) is the frequent references to you being away ill. Is it the bad leg that assaults you from time to time? Did you act as Secretary to him in the sense that Woodman acts as Secretary to me? If you only did all the filing and sorting, it would be invaluable.

I don't know if you would take the following as a compliment or an insult: the Church paper I take has an advertisement from another Journal called *Christianity Today* which says that any reader finding a new subscriber will receive a Free Copy of *The Best of C. S. Lewis*, value $5.95.[214] The offer closed on December 31st and I did not receive my copy until a

---

214 This special edition called *The Best of C. S. Lewis* (1969) contained five of Lewis's books collected in one volume: *The Screwtape Letters, The Great Divorce, Miracles, The Case for Christianity,* and *Christian Behavior.*

week ago, so I could not hope to receive it even if I did want to. As I have most of his writing, I do not think I would want it, except as a gift for someone else.

The TB and Leprosy world has been busier of late; the Diocesan Medical Coordinator work more demanding; and visitors more plentiful; so I have had little time. I did get a blessed weekend off at the Friary two weeks ago. I fully want to ride my motorbike, but the new pump I had ordered had not arrived (and <u>still</u> hasn't arrived) and the friend who tried to pump it up with a faulty pump let out more air than he put in. So I am still earthbound. Why it should take over a month for a commonly-used article like a pump to come a half-hour's flight over the mountains I do not know.

I must say that I am in sympathy with your housekeeper who refuses to go to Ireland, especially to Ulster. Unless one <u>must</u> face fighting, I should think it is common sense to keep away. However, you as a soldier would probably not agree. I did stay in Cornwall for a couple of days, with the Bishop of Truro and his family, since his daughter was the doctor relieving me, and they drove me from the calm, serene South to the stormy rocky North coast and I found it delightful. Failing your beloved island, I hope that you do go there. No doubt Summer still seems a long way away. I wonder if all the arrests that the police are making now will weed out the ring-leaders; or are there plenty more where they come from?

One of your brother's gifts to me is a desire to follow his example of patience in the face of interruptions, unwanted visitors, etc. Impatience is one of my deepest-rooted faults. He often seems to write about the virtue of exercising patience as one form of charity. I am at the moment being besieged by a woman who is most gifted at publicity and is devoted to the missionary cause. As a Mission needs publicity, we must be glad she is here. Her method is to pick some unfortunate individual missionary and build up a film strip round him (or her). It is my turn! She has pursued me with her camera (and given me all the extra slides, one or two of which you may see some day) and now is pursuing me to do the script, with fulsome flattery which will wear me down into vanity or mad temper before long. Moreover, as she is tied to the Territory for some weeks and has nowhere else much to stay, she looks like staying here. We also at the moment have a priest of the staff waiting to go to Port Moresby for surgery. He also is a loud and long talker, and I am unkindly turning each of them on to entertain the other while I get on with my work! Rosemary, our Secretary who is also doing the housekeeping, manages to keep a bubbling sense of humour, and so mealtimes are often accompanied by a ripple of laughter.

Christmas was very happy and pleasant. We had our service at 6:30 a.m. and our sister Hospital, St. Margaret's, had theirs at midnight. St. Margaret's Eroro, (the Secretary and her husband) and we joined forces at Oro Bay for a really opulent Christmas dinner, after a glorious swim in a sea that was like warm silk. We received a hamper from an unknown source before Christmas, but found out that the donor was a former member of staff. With the contents of that and other gifts we had a wonderful meal with a feeling of family unity that made it much more significant than most Christmas dinners.

I hope that you are feeling well in your midwinter, and finding life pleasant. I wonder if you ever plan to write other books? A pity to let your talent go to waste. Maybe the research necessary is too demanding?

yours affectionately,

# 61

26 January 1972

*[Note: This letter is handwritten by Warren Lewis, not typed]*

Dear Blanche,

I'm flattered at the invitation to use your Xtian name on the understanding that you will reciprocate with "Dear Warren."[215]

This alas isn't an answer to your letter but merely a note from a very tired man who has just emerged from hospital after an operation. When I heard that I must have a mechanical contrivance called a "pace maker" built into me to replace a defective blood pump, I said to myself "This is the end of the road for me"—no one more surprised than myself to find I felt no fear (of death that is, for of course fear of judgment is always with one). So "death's grim portal" isn't as bad as

---

215 The text we have of Biggs' letters is based on carbons she kept. These carbon copies bear no trace of an invitation to use first names. It is likely that this invitation was handwritten at the bottom of the letter after she finished typing it.

it is cracked up to be. Hospital complicated by an attack of a beastly virus infection called "Thrush" which is the sore throat to end all sore throats.

I'll try to write you a letter as soon as I get my strength back. Meanwhile,

Yours as ever,

Warren

# 62

6 February 1972

Dear Warren,

I feel much more comfortable now that we are Warren and Blanche! This also is not a proper answer to your letter received last Tuesday, but just to express concern that you have had another trip to Hospital, and for what might be called an exotic operation. I have never seen a pacemaker inserted as such things have been invented since I came to this out-of-the-way place. Once your heart has got used to obeying orders from a scrap of electricity, I should hope you would be much more comfortable and possibly more active. I hope and pray that it will prove so. I call it really bad luck that your sojourn in Hospital should have been complicated by an infection; maybe that is what is making you tired rather than the surgery itself.

With all the many people I have seen die, I have <u>almost</u> never seen anyone afraid of it, so far as an onlooker could tell. The Papuans particularly take it almost casually for themselves, although they have their fears of the spirits of others

218 | THE MAJOR & THE MISSIONARY

who have died, especially if the right thing has not been done by them at the time of death. I myself have only once faced what I thought was death—though quite likely I was nowhere near the "grim portal," and I had no fear, only regret at the thought of leaving my family and friends.[216] As time goes on and so many of our friends pass to the new life, the thought of death must become more acceptable to most of us, I think. A dear friend of mine died just two weeks ago—probably about your age—and we all think that it is a perfect, happy ending, as his health had just failed. He was Principal of our Teachers' Training College in this Diocese for twenty years. Someone once asked him rather slightingly what he thought he could teach these Papuans (most of them less than half-way through Primary School yet training to teach others!) and Oliver said, "I try to plant Christ in each one of my men"—and so he did. The Primate and the ex-Primate (his old Bishop and mine) both travelled especially to take part in his funeral.

I am writing in a hurry, as I go off for our Medical Committee tomorrow and after that will be kept busy on the correspondence to follow for a few weeks. There has been a fine old flutter to get the Committee together, since they must fly. We are just having a change of pilots for our Mission plane and so he is not available. Our Archdeacon is a pilot and has been trying to do the necessary flights, and then the plane he was using developed cracks and faults and he could

---

216 Biggs is most likely referring to her experience with tuberculosis. She contracted the disease during nursing school. After being quarantined in a Sanatorium for 6 months, Biggs moved back home to recuperate; it took six years.

not get another at the right time. However, they should all arrive in time, if we begin our meeting half a day late. There are plenty of problems, mostly those of lack of staff.

I hope that the next letter will assure me that you are feeling less tired, and that the new piece of anatomy will be a great success.

With my prayers.

# 61

17 February 1972

Dear Blanche,

Many thanks for yours of the 6th and I'm afraid this will be a very poor answer to it, for it is my fourth letter of the day, and I still tire very easily. The new electric pump—don't remember its proper name—seems to be working very satisfactorily; my doctor gave me a check yesterday and passed me as OK.

Fear of death. I once had a talk with a brother officer on that subject and he confessed that the prospect of dying terrified him. But as we went deeper into the subject what he really feared was <u>judgment</u>—and which of us can think of that without wishing that many things in our past had been left undone.

I wonder how I would react today to the smell of frangipani; the only association it has for me is that fifty years ago it was the favourite scent of those unhappy women who used to ply for hire in the Empire Music Hall in London.[217]

---

217 Frangipani, also known as plumeria, is a tropical plant with flowers known for their strong, sweet scent.

You seem to live in a perpetual state of dealing with crises of one kind or another and I am tickled at the thought of an Archdeacon/pilot—true, the Navy call their chaplains Sky Pilots, but that isn't quite the same thing! But perhaps more unexpected than the case of the Archdeacon is that of my dear friends the Roman Catholic nuns of Our Lady of Lourdes in Ireland. On their central African mission where the air is the only way to travel, all their pilots are <u>nuns</u>!

Life here is very unpleasant at the moment owing to the coal strike, which becomes worse instead of better; the Government seems helpless to do anything, tho' it is widely admitted that for the miners to cut off oil supplies to the electricity plants by "peaceful" picketing is illegal. The strike is of course a great nuisance domestically, for we are rationed for power—being at times cut off for as much as nine hours in the twenty-four.

Well I must stop now, for I've still a big accumulation of mail to deal with.

With all blessings, as ever.

Warren

# 64

22 February 1972

Dear Blanche,

I'm afraid I can't make this a letter, but I must let you have a line to say that I'm delighted with your Christmas gift which arrived last week, and in perfect order in spite of the time which it has been on the road. I, or should I say, we are delighted with it and it now adorns the place of honour on top of the TV set! I've seen one of these boats in the flesh so speak, but cannot remember where—Singapore, Columbo? I was told they were catamarans.[218]

Our coal strike is officially over, but we are warned that the emergency will continue until the end of March which is not a very cheerful prospect.[219] The thing is a great nuisance; for instance yesterday, our worst day, we were cut off from

---

218 A catamaran is a type of craft with two parallel hulls, connected by an arching frame that supports and balances the body of the boat.

219 This coal strike ended on February 19, 1972, after the miners accepted a settlement. This capitulation was partly prompted when an official state of emergency was declared on February 2.

power from 3 p.m. to six p.m. and from 9 p. m. to mid-night—how jolly in a house where we cook by electricity!

With renewed thanks and all best wishes, as ever,

Warren

## 65

5 March 1972

Dear Warren,

You are treating me very well with two letters written within five days of each other. But I hope you do not drive yourself to write when you feel tired; and please don't feel bound to answer this until you feel energetic enough. I would not like our correspondence to be a burden to you. I am glad you are pleased with the canoe. I am never sure whether a catamaran has two hulls or one; I have read of (but not seen) a trimaran which had three.

Men who strike always choose the time when their strike will give a maximum of trouble and discomfort; I wonder to what extent the strike comes to an end because of wives nagging to their striking husbands about <u>their</u> discomfort? In the dead of winter, I should think discomfort is too mild a word to use. What sort of heating do you have? Probably wood or coal fires are banned because of air pollution; if gas is not obtainable there isn't much left. I hope that things are returning to normal now. It all probably lengthens the period of your recovery.

Re: fear of death: I wonder if your fear (and the fear of your brother officers) as fear of Judgment is made more real by the Victorian attitudes in which they were brought up? My impression is that the boys of the late 1890s had stern parents and the father-son relationship held a good deal of fear and sense of guilt, which is quite missing from such a relationship nowadays. My own father was strict, but he was well on in his forties when I was born and so was mellowing; he also was not nearly so stern with his daughters as with his sons. I have almost no fear of judgment which I think may be due to the gentler upbringing I had. No doubt it is a fault in me and some day I may wake up with a jerk to my failings in that regard. Yet my everyday puny repentance of sins does not seem to carry me over into a fear of judgment. From the little I can know of my contemporaries' attitudes, I would say they have no fear of judgment either.

I discovered a new book and a new writer at the Friary recently. The book was *Blessing Unbounded: A Vision* by Harry Blamires. He has written a trilogy on Hell, Purgatory, and Heaven—the one I read, of course. It is very good and somewhat in the Charles Williams tradition. I wonder if you have come across them?[220]

Frangipani: you surprise me when you say that the "ladies of light virtue" were able to procure them in cold old London; also that you would not have lived among them in your

---

220 Harry Blamires (1916-2017) was an English author, theologian, and literary critic. This trilogy comprises *Devil's Hunting Ground, Cold War in Hell,* and *Highway to Heaven.*

African days. They grow very readily here and their perfume on a moonlit night is sheer joy. They are to New Guinea what roses are to a temperate climate.

I think I have heard of your nun friends who are sky-pilots too! New Guinea has a saintly Roman Catholic Archbishop who pilots himself among the mountains, says his office while he flies, just looking up occasionally to tilt the nose of the plane away from the mountains. They say that Govt. officials whom he might take with him shiver in their shoes and would prefer a little more attention to the flight and less to the Lord.

I am now in Port Moresby for a Committee meeting of our Combined Churches Medical Council, which has gone gloriously agley.[221] The Chairman is our charming American nun (a doctor) who does not fly herself around her domain but bestrides a motorbike; she also is said to climb mountains and down gullies that patrol officers find too difficult. She is spending today in Retreat so I have not been able to speak to her; two members of the Committee are having medical treatment in Sydney, one doctor called me on the radio to say he could not possibly get in, and that leaves only 3 of us. We will have to have a brief talk and arrange to have a proper Executive meeting later. Meanwhile I am seeing a TB specialist, and (I hope) the Leprosy one; the Public Health Department is much too slow in paying our subsidy; and I had a long session with the Bishop last night about our Medical policy etc.

Our Bishop aged 53, the Archbishop of Sydney, aged over 60, and a "Bishop" of the United Church, (45) who was

---

221 "Agley" means askew or awry.

batman to the Archbishop when he was here as an Army Chaplain, are all going to walk the infamous Kokoda Trail to raise money for the Diocese.[222] Do you have these Walkathons in England? People sponsor them and pay an agreed amount for each mile that is walked. The Bishop's plan to do it in ten days (the Army in fit condition take 7) and it is a wicked trail up and down terrible mountains.[223] The Bishop plans to invite one of our medical men to go with them, ready to give first aid if necessary. My chief concern is snakebite, though snakes do not seem to have been a menace to the army when they fought there.[224] It is especially good that Sydney is joining in, as that Diocese is the last stronghold of all that is understood by Protestant Anglicanism, while we in New Guinea stand for "Catholic" Anglicanism. So it is a wonderful gesture of Archbishop Loan to do this for our Diocese. They hope that the Sydney Diocese will really support the walk. A strange way to help on the work of the Church!

---

222 During the First World War, officers in the British army were assigned soldier-servants who performed a number of duties, including driving, conveying messages, acting as bodyguards, and maintaining the officer's uniform. In the inter-war years, this British orderly became known as a "batman."

223 The Kokoda Trail is a 60-mile trail running through the Owen Stanley Mountain Range in the south of Papua New Guinea.

224 Papua New Guinean hospitals report some of the highest snakebite rates in the world, and, due to the large rural population, there are likely many additional cases that go unreported. There are five species of venomous snakes in Papua New Guinea that pose serious risk to humans. Natives term any dark snake the "Papuan Black," which they carefully avoid.

One of our Assistant Bishops, Bevan Meredith, has gone off to England for a few weeks on a free flight.[225] Qantas are starting a new flight between New Guinea (and Australia of course) and Britain and gave 70 free return tickets to residents of the Territory, favouring Missions, businessmen and including 30 indigenous people. Bishop Bevan was chosen for us, and as it is his first trip it is very nice. I don't suppose <u>he</u> will turn up in Oxford to preach?

We had dinner at the Friary below this house last night. They have pictures of their various Houses, and one is of St. Benet's Church Cambridge. Have you ever worshipped there? I believe that your brother used to "drop in" on the Cambridge Friars in the old days.

I <u>have</u> chatted on! Don't let me be a nuisance to you, if you are below par.

Yours affectionately,

---

225 Bishop Meredith was an Australian who originally went to New Guinea to teach but found his calling in the church. He later became the Archbishop of the Anglican Church of New Guinea, serving 1990-1996.

# 66

14 March 72

Dear Madam,

The Major thanks you for your letter. But regrets not being well enough to answer it. As you can be sure he will do so as soon as feels well enough.

 Yours.

 Len Miller

# 67

16 April 1972

My dear Warren,

It was kind of you to ask your Mr. Miller to write and let me know that you had received my last letter. This letter is not meant to worry you into thinking that I expect you to answer, but just to let you know that I am remembering you in my prayers (such as they are) and wondering how you are. Perhaps Mr. Miller could send me a note again to let me know how you are progressing, if in Hospital or out of it—and if you are being well looked after; It looks as if the fine bit of electricity they put inside you is not quite as wonderful as we hoped!

I hope you are getting some Spring and well enough to see it and enjoy it. You Britishers are lucky in celebrating Easter in Spring, whereas we have it just as Autumn is getting under way. Our Easter went off peacefully and quietly with a service at 6:30 a.m. taken by our new Papuan priest who is really stirring up our Parish. We also had a special offering for our sister Diocese of Melanesia which suffered colossal damage from cyclones, one at each end of the stretch of islands making up the Diocese.[226] On some islands every Church and priest's house was ruined, and in some cases whole villages destroyed, gardens, coconuts and all.

Life is busy as usual and I am a bit of a dull girl from too much work and too little playing and/or praying. I hope to get away to a short Retreat next weekend.

I hope that you are comfortable and not in pain, and that there are plenty of people to care for you and your needs.

Yours affectionately,

---

226 Three cyclones hit Melanesia during this time: Carlotta (January 5-21), Wendy (January 30 through February 9), and Emily (March 27 through April 4).

# 68

24 April 1972

Dear Blanche,

Many thanks for your kind note of the 16th with its enquiries about my health. Well, the great thing is that I'm in no pain and when one considers the "might have been"! But the fits of dizziness continue and are a considerable nuisance, confining me to the house or its immediate vicinity as they do; still, at my age I don't want much exercise anyway. So you can say all is well. And I'm well looked after, which is more than many, perhaps the majority, of old people in this country can say.

How very queer, how distracting it must be to keep Easter in the autumn—even more bizarre than the Australian Christmas which I understand falls in the height of summer. I wonder what sort of weather it would have been in Jerusalem on the first (and subsequent) Easter Days? But at least I take it that autumn is less emphatic with you than it is in northern latitudes; I'm going by my own recollection of the tropics in Africa where the jungle was much the same quilt of dull dirty green the whole year round. I've never met a cyclone but used to be familiar with typhoons which are I suppose first cousins to cyclones. Sad about the destruction in Melanesia.

Here we wallow in our usual sea of industrial troubles of which the most irritating at the moment is what is inaccurately described as the railway "strike". Really it is a "work to rule", which means meticulous inspections normally ignored, as for instance examinations of the screws supporting curtains in the coaches.[227] But the public has begun to take the bit in its teeth; last week a homeward bound commuter train pulled up eight miles short of the destined terminus and the driver announced (I forget the pretext) that he was going no further—whereupon the commuters dragged him out of his cab and with fists and feet "persuaded" him to complete the journey! Then we have a dock strike up North, but this the new Industrial Court has [been] dealt with pretty promptly—by fining the striking Union £55,000; it's one of the wealthy unions, but even so they won't be able to pay that sum out of the petty cash drawer.[228] And on top of it all is the continuing runny sore of my poor Ulster; but this doesn't bear talking about.

You may be a "dull girl" in the flesh, though I doubt it, and hope that some day I may be able to satisfy that such is not the case; but on paper you may be assured that you aren't.

---

227 In April of 1972, the railway union rejected the British Railway Board's offer of an 11% raise. Rather than call a strike, they initiated a "work-to-rule": employees perform the minimum requirements of their contracts and no more.

228 The dock strike continued until August, 1972, when the unions settled for less than what they had previously demanded.

I trust you were refreshed by the Retreat.

    Yours affectionately,

    Warren

# 69

28 May 1972

My dear Warren,

You can guess how pleased I was to get your note, written by yourself, which was reassuring in itself. However, you are clearly still having to take care of yourself in a way that is irksome. I thank God that you have no pain or great handicap and that you have your Mr. and Mrs. Miller (am I right?) to look after you. As summer is almost upon you, maybe you are able to get out a bit. Though from what little I have heard of the English weather, it is rain sufficient to wash out the Cricket Australia versus sundry English teams.

Work has been pretty fierce lately and I have not been able to keep in touch with my friends. In spite of good resolutions, the weeks have gone by without my writing to you. The last time I wrote of cyclones in our sister Diocese of Melanesia, and in North Queensland. I saw Bishop John Chisholm of Melanesia a few weeks ago and he said that, when he went back again soon after the cyclone, in all the villages the first thing the people rebuilt was their <u>Church</u>—even before their own houses. Is there a congregation anywhere else in the world that would do that? Now our Papua has "copped it"; on Ascension Day our next-door Station, about 60 miles away, was absolutely destroyed. By a miracle, although about 4,000 people are homeless and bits of houses flew in all directions, there was only one life lost—with a rumour of a second. We have had about 100 evacuees, wives and children, settled in this Hospital until new homes can be built for them. The Government supplies us with food for them, and we look after them.[229] Now two babies have developed whooping cough, and I dread to hear what may be happening in Tufi in hopeless villages, if other babies are going to get it. The immunizations have obviously not been kept up maybe because the staff did not do it or because the people would not bring their children for injections.

If silence means no news, England must be having a rest from strikes just now. You poor things, it does seem to be one thing after another. Australia has even more than England, but they do not last long, I suppose because the authorities give in to the strikers' demands more readily. A couple of years ago, New Guinea decided to fall into the fashion and the students in a Teachers' Training College struck for better conditions. That ended almost before it began: I fancy the authorities said, "Get back to work or get out of the service!"

Poor Ireland; every news session seems to have more news of trouble there: as you say, it does not bear thinking about;

---

229 The destruction was caused by Severe Tropical Cyclone Hannah, which lasted from May 8 to 11, 1972, and ravaged the town of Tufi and the surrounding areas.

and Vietnam is much, much worse.

Your thought that a Summer Christmas and an Autumn Easter are bizarre sounds strange to us, who have never had it otherwise. You should have included the Southern Hemisphere in your wanderings! As for Jerusalem at Easter, I should imagine that an early Easter would be Springlike, but a later one more like Summer. I was in Nazareth for Ascension Day, May 8th if I remember rightly and it was quite fiercely hot in the day, but cold enough at night for a hot water bottle for a cold mortal like me. And Jerusalem a few days later was similar. By the Lake of Galilee the hillsides were truly "white already to harvest" even in May.[230] The crops growing by the lake were not yellow like our wheat and barley, but shining white and very tall. They seemed to have been planted almost casually, with no fences or boundaries.

I have had a visit to Port Moresby to join our Combined Churches Medical Executive in talks with the Public Health Department, among other things helping to plan a National Health Service, so we hope to avoid some of the mistakes made by other countries; and the Director visited us to talk about the future of St. Luke's, among other things. He has "given us notice" to close by the middle of next year and has invited The Anglican Mission to run the TB & Leprosy programme for the whole Northern District. That means B. B. until she retires, with as many Mission staff as she can muster. The Mission has accepted the plan to move out by June 30th

---

230 A reference to John 4:35: "Say not ye, There are yet four months, and then cometh harvest? behold, I say unto you, Lift up your eyes, and look on the fields; for they are white already to harvest" (KJV).

next year, and is considering the other development. For me personally, that means two things: I can take my leave when it is due towards the end of the year; and I cannot in honesty take time off, or resign, in mid-year 1973 to take my long-planned trip to England. It would mean going the following year. I have many regrets about this, and one of them is the need to postpone meeting you for another year (if then); but it is clear to me that it is the will of God for me. We have been muddling along for so long wondering what the future of our work is to be, so this is a relief. I could not have carried on without some sort of holiday until next year; even now I may have to take a week off—if I can find a week somewhere in the calendar!

A sobering thing happened last weekend. A girl who works with the Education Department but was previously on our staff rides a motorbike like mine. Last Monday she rode off to work in pouring rain and somehow skidded and fell off and fractured her skull, even though she had a crash helmet on. She is improving now. It was not, as far as one can see, carelessness or (certainly not) drunkenness. However, I suppose one can't let it influence one's own riding, when that riding is necessary to the work. But I do pick my weather.

I saw in an old *Illustrated London News* that Tolkien of the Rings fame received an Honour from the Queen, and there was a picture of him.[231] How many of the Inklings are

---

231 Tolkien was awarded the honor of a CBE, or Commander of the Most Excellent Order of the British Empire, from Queen Elizabeth II at Buckingham Palace in March of 1972. This rank is one below knighthood, awarded for leadership or service rendered regionally or

left? And did they ever meet in Cambridge or only in Oxford?

Do look after yourself; and I hope these giddy fits are passing; and that the pacemaker is pacemaking in a satisfactory way.

With all good wishes and my prayers,

---

nationally. Three years later, on January 1, 1975, Biggs was awarded an OBE, or Officer of the Most Excellent Order of the British Empire. An OBE is granted to those who have performed admirable service in the arts, sciences, public services, or philanthropy.

# 70

6 June 1972

Dear Blanche,

Many thanks for yours of 28th May. So far here there has been no summer—fires every day etc.—and what is worse, the weather people hold out no hope of any summer coming; which is hard on us old 'uns. As for my health, it's much the same, continuing dizzy fits and the consequent immobilization. But after all, I've got little to complain of. Mrs. Miller is I am sorry to say far from well, but Mr. Miller is proving a tower of strength—has turned into an excellent cook amongst other things. I'm rather down in the dumps this morning—all set to visit my beloved Ireland on the 11th for a fortnight, and our miserable beast of a car has broken down. So the whole plan is in ruins, and so vanishes my last chance to see Ireland once again—for I would be optimistic if I reckoned on being alive in the summer of 1973.

I was sorry to hear your cyclone news, but as far as I can see things might have been very much worse. My own terror in the way of these phenomena would be a volcanic eruption or an earthquake; but I don't think either of these come your way.

How very interesting about Palestinian conditions. I had always imagined that "white for the harvest" was a mistranslation of some word in the original and lo and behold it is a fact; aesthetically considered I should think white corn would be less satisfying than the golden of these latitudes.

Strikes? Don't you believe it. At the moment we have a railway "go slow" which is almost as much of a nuisance as a downright strike; and we are apparently about to have a dock strike, which will be a disaster for the export trade. Then there is the food crisis. Apparently there is a world shortage of beef, with the result that steak is now selling here at £1.00 a pound! I need hardly add that steak has disappeared from The Kilns bill of fare!

Then violence and disorder is on the increase. We had a hideous case here this week when a girl infant asleep in her pram in the garden was stabbed to death with fifty knife wounds by a woman whom the police have caught. I suppose the verdict will be "guilty but insane". My doctor tells me that she was probably an unbalanced woman who had lost her own only child at birth. Apparently when this happens a woman can go right round the bend.

A National Health Service has its uses and its drawbacks, amongst the latter being that the GP has become a mere forwarding agent for the hospitals; he just hasn't time to cope with his huge list of patients. A minor trouble for him is that his consulting room has become a women's morning gossip rendezvous, filled with ladies whose complaints are either trivial or imaginary. Still, the setup has come to stay, and its benefits outweigh its abuses.

Yes, Tolkien has collected a CBE. The Inklings never met at Cambridge, always at Oxford, and the ghost of them survives. Every year we have a get-together of my brother's old friends at which we drink to his memory. This year it is being held on the 5th of next month at his old College, Magdalen, and I hope to be fit enough to attend.

I'm sorry indeed to hear of the uncertainty of your future and hope that the position will be clearer when next you write.

With all good wishes, as ever,

Warren

## 71

25 June 1972

My dear Warren,

It was very good to receive your letter of June 6th—just ten days before your birthday. I fancy that you and the recently deceased Duke of Windsor would have been about the same age. The Duke as Prince of Wales was a sort of hero of mine (the power of the Press, no doubt!) and I will never forget the turmoil and sadness I went through at the time of the abdication.[232]

I am sorry for your disappointment over losing your trip to Ireland. However, maybe the breakdown of the car was "meant"! Ireland is a very unhealthy place for even casual travelers, I should think. The visit would have saddened you in any case. As for 1973, one cannot really know what it may bring. You seem to have the ability to accept whatever it may bring you. I still hope that you and I may both live on this

---

232 Edward VIII abdicated his position as King of England in order to marry American socialite Wallis Simpson, a woman twice divorced. He received the title Duke of Windsor.

earth long enough to meet some day, but if we do not meet here, I expect that we will meet in the next life.

Steak! Australia exports millions of tons of it, but America gets the lion's share, I believe. Is your £1 per pound paid for locally grown meat or imported, I wonder? Our little Popondetta has recently opened its first butcher's shop selling almost entirely beef products from a local plantation. They have grown rubber for years and then went in for beef cattle which graze under the rubber trees. The best steak is about one dollar (50 pence of your money?) But the imported meat is more expensive, especially as it has to be brought into the country under strictly frozen conditions.

Each man has his own special terror, I suppose. It is surprising that yours is earthquakes and/or volcanoes. We have lots of earth tremors and parts of the Territory fairly often have a quake that brings some destruction. We had a volcanic eruption in 1951 which blew out the side of our Mount Lamington and killed 4000 people.[233] I was on leave at the time, but flew back to help in the aftermath. We had over 1000 refugees at Oro Bay for some weeks and our Hospital took in the sick ones—mostly dysentery and women in childbirth. I think the disaster that would make me most fearful would be fire.

Life is busy, with a multiplicity of demands and interests. It is depressing that one <u>never</u> catches up! However, one must

---

233 Mount Lamington can be easily seen from Popondetta. It was not recognized as a volcano before it erupted in 1951. As it was not considered active, authorities did not evacuate the surrounding villages, and this decision was directly responsible for the unusually high death toll.

do what one can and leave the rest. One of our Tufi evacuees took ill last night and died at 2:30 this morning, so I am short on sleep. The silly old man refused any treatment when he first came when we might have been able to help him, and it was only when he was semi-conscious that we could even try to help him; and then it was too late. My right-hand man is his nephew and has to be away from duty today to try and arrange a charter flight to take the body home to Tufi for burial. First, he must find a rich relative with enough money to pay for it! Meanwhile my sick patients here are in the care of much less experienced medicals.

I hope that you get to the Inklings reunion on the 5th. Is the date of any special significance?

Herewith a couple of photographs of myself. One is never satisfied with one's own pictures.

## 72

4 July 1972

*[Note: This letter is handwritten rather than typed.]*

Dear Blanche,

Many thanks for yours of 25th June and more particularly for the photos, which expose you as a fraud! So often you talk of your retirement that I'd pictured you an elderly woman, and behold, you disclose yourself of merely entering upon middle age—from my point on the road a mere youngster whom I must begin to patronize!

Like so many people you have a distorted view of the Ireland of to-day; provided you don't go within ten miles of the Ulster border, you are as safe or safer over there than you are in Birmingham or Liverpool. Yes, the collapse of the holiday was a sad business, but I'm now cogitating a revised version of it—a fortnight in the hospital of Our Lady of Lourdes amongst my delightful nuns.[234] Do you know anything about

---

234 Lewis made numerous visits to Our Lady of Lourdes in Drogheda, Ireland, a Catholic hospital located just north of Dublin. The first was

conventual life? Before I'd stopped at Lourdes I thought of it as sad and silent, whereas laughter and gaiety are the keynotes of a convent or at any rate of this one. Of course, I don't expect them to cure me, but at least I shall get what I need so badly and cannot get here. The season has come when camera-clad Americans descend on me wanting to know what was my brother's favourite breakfast food, his views on the unmarried mother, etc. etc.; and in addition the steady two hours a day six days a week letter answering—not made any easier by the fact that just now I'm too shaky to use a typewriter. (But don't take this as a hint to you not to write!) The beef I talked about was Scotch, the best on our market, but as for the money value no one knows. Since the £ was allowed to "float" it has dropped 7½ percent both in New York & Berlin.

No, no earthquakes for me. I'm familiar with both the tornado & the typhoon—don't think you have either do you?—and they are quite sufficient examples of Nature's exuberance for me!

There is no special significance in the Inklings reunion date, it is merely that coming in the middle of the "Long Vacation" it is convenient for academic people.[235] I alas am far too shaky to attend this time—the first of these reunions

---

in 1947, when the nuns nursed him to health after a bout of binge drinking.

235 The school year at Oxford University is divided into three terms: Michaelmas (fall), Hilary (spring), Trinity (summer). The break between the end of the Trinity Term and the beginning of Michaelmas Term is the longest, and so it is called the long vacation or the "long vac."

I shall have missed.

Summer is apparently going to pass us over entirely this year. June was the second worst June since official records began to be kept, and so far July shows no sign of improving on June's detestable record.[236] Yes, I hope I live to meet you, but in the meantime all blessings attend you.

As ever,

Warren

---

236 June of 1972 in England was an unusually chilly month, with temperatures consistently below average, the coldest June since 1916. The highest temperature reached in Oxford that month was 20.4° C, or 68° F.

# 73

13 August 1972

My dear Warren,

I have been slow in answering your last letter of July 4th, as I have been away a good deal, at Conferences etc. They are very interesting and stimulating, but do not leave time for other pursuits. I wonder if you have been to Lourdes? You may be there now. I can imagine what a blessing and refreshment such a visit will be to you, whether or not you receive physical benefit from it. I hope for the latter too, of course. We have discussions here about faith healing and some of our number consider it a lack of faith not to expect healing just as one prays for it. I cannot agree, and know in my own experience that benefit always results, but may be an ability to accept with courage the fact that one may not improve physically. Yes, I can well believe that the Convent is a place of laughter. You would no doubt choose the time of your visit to escape from the tourists. Surely no other country has "tourists" who ask such stupid questions as the Americans? Or is it just that the Americans are more numerous and so have a higher probability of having stupid people among them? I am so sorry you had to miss your Inklings reunion. I have just been re-reading Dietrich Bonhoeffer's *Letters and Papers from Prison*, and suppose that you have read them also? What a faith he had to keep his charity and sanity at so high a pitch through his long imprisonment.[237] His picture of the future working of the Church is coming very true too, in the oecumenical area. I also read recently *The Tartan Pimpernel*, the story of a Presbyterian minister who helped Allied troops to escape through Marseilles. When he was imprisoned and treated (at least for a time) much worse than Bonhoeffer was, he kept his faith and his sanity by interceding desperately for his fellow workers and fellow-sufferers.[238]

You flatter me by saying I am entering middle-age: remember I am only 15 years younger than you, so that, if I am young, you are correspondingly young, too. We have our former Bishop, aged 73, staying with us now, on what he thinks is his last visit to the Territory. He was the Bishop of New Guinea for 26 years and I served under him for half of them.[239] He also is an Oxford man. He keeps telling us he is

---

237 Dietrich Bonhoeffer was held in various military prisons and concentration camps for two years. His imprisonment lasted from April of 1943 to April of 1945, when he was executed by Hitler for his complicity in an assassination attempt against the Führer.

238 Rev. Dr. Donald Currie Caskie helped approximately 2,000 Allied military men to escape from France. Though he spent the latter half of the war in prison, he returned home to Scotland and to pastoral ministry after peace was declared.

239 This is most likely Bishop Philip Strong. For more, see footnote 4.

an old man, but he plunges into services and meetings with his old energy, even though he soon tires and has to go and rest. This morning I bounced into Eroro for the service, 1½ hours long, when he both celebrated and preached, then shook hands with hundreds of people before retiring to drink some tea. I say, I bounced, to give you some idea of the state of the road. The season is too dry for the Public Works Department to do anything about the road until we have some good rains. You could send us some of yours with mutual profit!

We also this week had a visit from the Administrator of the Territory and his wife. We were asked to invite a few people and provide morning tea. It all went off very nicely, with a good mixture of brown and white people. But it would happen when we have V. I. P. visitors, that our water-pump had broken down and we had no water-supply! It took the Public Works people 24 hours to come and fix it; and then, like the usual plumber, they had forgotten to bring an essential spare part (though I had notified them on the radio that this was what was wrong) and had to go back the 23 miles to Popondetta to get it! And so public funds are wasted.

We have been getting some very sick new patients in lately, who arrive like little skeletons. It is one of the joys of this work to see them fill out and begin to take an interest in life. Apart from these more dramatic successes, the TB and leprosy work is rather monotonous, medically speaking. I have had a rude reminder this week that leprosy is likely to be a lifelong disease. Two young men were brought back, one of whom had officially completed his treatment, and the other had stopped taking it himself; this after about 3-4 years of treatment. Both have become active again. The younger sister of one has just developed signs of it as well. She has been clear of it on previous inspections. And so the work boils down to a constant hunting for signs of active disease in people who might consider themselves clear of it.

We also got in a family from West Irian—the western end of this large island, which was taken over from the Dutch some years ago. These people are refugees and have permissive residence. The husband has been making political trouble among his fellow refugees, but his wife and two children have tuberculosis; so the powers that be have sent them here where it is quiet, away from the opportunities of making trouble. He seems a pleasant enough chap, and we have found him a job here. They belong to the Dutch Reformed Church and seem glad to attend our services. But the District Commissioner says that at the first sign of political activity they will be sent back home where the young man would promptly be killed. It is hard to know what does go on over the border, but there was certainly some persecution when the country was first taken over.

I do not know how far it is stern duty that makes you write letters so conscientiously when you find it so demanding; and how far it is carrying on a hobby that might well be dropped. More likely, it is your form of service to your neighbor. I am sorry you do find it burdensome. I certainly love receiving your letters, but please do not let me be a burden.

Yours affectionately,

# 74

13 October 1972

*[Note: This letter is handwritten rather than typed.]*

Dear Miss Biggs,

I am sorry to have to tell you the Major is in Hospital in Ireland and not at all well. Quite unable to answer any letters. You can be sure he will write to you as soon as he is well enough.

Yours sincerely,
Len Miller

75

15 October 1972

My dear Warren,

Your nice Mr. Miller wrote to let me know that you are in
Hospital in Ireland, and I hope that he will forward this on. I
have been anxious to know how you are and am sad to know
that you are still in Hospital. However, it will be a comfort
to you to be back in your beloved Ireland once more, even if
your views of Ireland are bounded by the walls of a Hospital
ward.

In spite of my own long silence, you have been much in
my thoughts and prayers. I wonder how long you were in
Lourdes, if you did eventually go there: if you did, I know
that you would receive some benefit from your visit; if not
physical, then spiritual for certain. It appears that that pacemaker is not the answer to your physical problems.

Life for me has been very busy, with lots of new worries—if worry is a sin, then I am a pretty bad sinner!—and
adapting to changing circumstances. This Hospital is to
close in the middle of next year, but I myself am to move out

after my leave, which I hope will begin before Christmas, but even that is not certain. I shall live in a Government house in Popondetta, do much more traveling than I do at the moment, and visit this Hospital just once a week. That leaves the responsibility of the Hospital on the shoulders of my Papuan nurse in charge. He is the best man available for it, but even so, he has his limitations.

In September, life was made interesting by a visit from a luxury cruise of Anglicans visiting our Diocese. Lots of my friends were on board, and my own sister [Win] decided to come. Many of the cruise people were in their 60s, 70s and 80s (they tell me one was in her 90s), people who had been working and giving for the Diocese all through the years. From the expense point of view the Diocese will about break even, but in goodwill and renewed interest the benefits are very great. The Bishop, our Publicity Officer, and two attractive Papuan girls were hosts to the passengers. Both girls I have known almost since babyhood. My sister flew over from Port Moresby to spend a weekend with me, and on the Monday I flew back with her, joined the ship and came with her from Moresby, visiting Dogura and here at Oro Bay, then on to Lae. By that means I had a chance of seeing my friends. It was a delightful interlude, interlarded with work when in port. The trip to Lae was for a meeting of Bishops and Heads of Divisions (I am head of the medical Division) to see just how many more dollars we could cut off our Budget!

I have had another spell of wakefulness at night, and have been re-reading *The Great Divorce*, and find it very satisfying as an explanation of Divine justice and Divine love.

If and when you feel fit to write again, I shall be very glad to receive a letter, but do not push yourself into writing before you do feel well again. I would be glad if Mr. Miller could let me know how you are.

With my prayers always, Yours affectionately,


P. S. One old friend on the tour, who must be over 80, told me that she had prayed for me every single day since I first came to the Diocese. Isn't it staggering? No wonder the strength comes when we need it.

# 76

*[undated]*

*[Note: This letter is handwritten rather than typed.]*

Dear Madam,

Am sorry to say the Major was taken ill whilst on holiday and
has been unable to answer any mail. I am pleased to say he is
getting better and will write to you as soon as he is fit enough.
Yours,
L. Miller

*[undated]*

Dear Miss Biggs,

I am pleased to say the Major is slowly improving still not well enough to answer letters and still in Hospital in Ireland.[240] I am going to see him next week hoping to find him well enough for me to make arrangements for me fetch him home.

    Yours sincerely

    L. Miller

---

240 While in hospital, Warren developed gangrene in both feet, necessitating surgery.

78

5 November 1972

Dear Mr. Miller,

Thank you very much for writing to me at various times to let me know how the Major is. I have been anxious to know and am very glad to know that he is improving. Perhaps you are now in Ireland getting ready to bring him home. I know that you always see that he has what he needs.

I would be grateful if you will continue from time to time to let me know how his health is, if he is not fit to write himself. I plan to go on leave in a month or so, and from the middle of December my address will be c/o Miss W. Biggs, "Burville," 4 Swanston Street, New Town, Hobart, Tasmania, 7008.[241]

Please give Major Lewis my very warm greetings,
Yours sincerely,
(Miss) or (Doctor) B. Biggs.
It doesn't matter which!

---

241 Win's House was called Burville (a family name).

## 79

Burville Christmas Eve 1972

My dear Warren,

I would like to have had a letter to you arriving in time for Christmas, but it could not be done. I have been thinking of you and wondering if you are feeling better; and how you are standing up to England's winter.

I arrived home on leave last Wednesday, my 63rd birthday, in a heat wave; now we are having wind, rain, with patches of sunshine, cold and even snow on the mountain. It sounds so much colder to hear that it is Zero, Celsius, than to hear it is 32 degrees, Fahrenheit. This is the season of yachting, but they had to cancel all the river sports yesterday because of the rough conditions.

It is very good to be at home, and to drop all the responsibilities and demands of St. Luke's. One has to get away to be able to sit lightly to things: but I still find that I cannot sit and do nothing, but have the constant urge to use every minute of the day. But it is pleasant to do the things one <u>wants</u> to do, and not the things one <u>has</u> to do.

One of the nice things about being 63 is that I mean to apply for an old age pension. One of our staff has just returned from leave and he got the pension without any trouble, so I am going to apply too. It should bring me in as much, if not more, than I receive from the Mission and will save the Mission the cost of keeping me. As we had a 20% cut in our budget for the coming year, that will be all the more welcome. I learned just how much one can prune a budget and still keep the major work going. We had to cut out allowances for equipment and some maintenance, and we have postponed Synod until 1974 with its preparatory Regional Conferences, and that saves some thousands of dollars.

My sister and I have been to the Cathedral by taxi this morning, and will go again to the midnight service, if we keep to our plan; but a midnight service with rain and cold is not too attractive.[242] Are you able to go to Church, I wonder? Or will you have your Christmas Communion in your own house? I hope that you will have friends to visit you (but not too many) to keep you cheerful.

Wishing you a New Year of better health and greater happiness,

Yours affectionately,

---

242 Biggs is referring to St. David's Cathedral, the principal Anglican cathedral in Hobart. Blanche's sisters Lil and Win served here so faithfully that after they died, two chancel chairs were dedicated to them in a ceremony on December 1, 1986. The chairs are still used in the Cathedral Chapel.

## 80

17 January 73

Dear Miss Biggs,

The Major is still in Hospital in Ireland and still not well enough to answer letters. I go to see him every month. He had quite a good Christmas. He says he hopes you are enjoying your leave and still hopes that he will soon be well enough to write to you.

Yours sincerely
Len Miller

# 81

Burville 12 February 1973

My dear Warren,

It was good of your Mr. Miller to write again and let me know of your progress. I wonder if you are still in Hospital and still in Ireland? He says that you had a good Christmas, which I hope means that you were well enough to enjoy it. How much enjoyment of anything depends on one's state of health and also of one's mood! The news as it reaches us is very depressing; maybe for one who is so close to it the grim part is diluted with more humdrum events.[243] I hope that you will soon return to Oxford and be able to take up some more threads of your life. Do you have the energy to read, I wonder?

My leave is almost over; thank you for your good wishes for it, transmitted by Mr. Miller. It has been of mixed good, by which I mean that I don't feel as revivified as I hoped and expected. Maybe it is physical, maybe it has other causes.

---

243 Political violence continued to plague Northern Ireland, with riots and bombings occurring almost weekly.

We have had a spate of relations visiting us and we have visited them, and being social is NOT my cup of tea. A simple afternoon of chatting to people with whom I have little in common leaves me tired and dull; yet the same time spent with my dear friends is not nearly so tiring. However, I have had many days of what I am pleased to call "puddling", which means doing what I like to do: reading, sewing, listening to music, shopping—and a fair amount of picnicking, going to concerts and a theatre or two. It is good to be at home during the small-fruit season, and strawberries and raspberries have been very good, as well as peaches and apricots. These are things one does not see in New Guinea.

There is a lot of publicity going on in connection with the Eucharistic Congress soon to take place in Melbourne. Australia has two new Cardinals and they did hope that the Pope would come out, but he will not do so. The chief point of interest from our point of view is that the theme of the Congress is oecumenism, and "Protestants" of all kinds are taking part; our own Primate among them.[244]

I find life in "civilization" very confusing and saddening; the whole basis of everyone's thinking (and I find my own also) seems to be money. In New Guinea one is sheltered from much of it because of our unsophisticated people; but here money and all it implies is an obsession. I suppose people who live here live with it, and do not notice it so much. In many ways it will be good to get back to more simple ways.

---

244 The 40th Eucharistic Congress was held in Melbourne, Australia, February 18-25. Its theme was "Love one another as I have loved you," taken from John 13:34.

In other ways, life will be much more difficult in the coming year. I am to have a few days at Avalon, the home of a fairly new Community of Anglicans, and that will I hope give me time and opportunity to "tune in" to the new life I will have in Popondetta.[245] By the way, the old St. Luke's address will be correct for the next few months; even after St. Luke's closes in June, the old address would still find me; but I will have to let you know which is the best new one.

Your Mr. Miller points out that your own Oxford address is slightly altered, to Lewis Close. That is a very good way to remember a man or a family, unpretentious and likely to be permanent.

On Christmas Eve my sister and I watched the choir of King's College, Cambridge, singing Carols on television; it was glorious. I suppose you have often attended services in that Chapel, as your life has been pretty closely linked with Cambridge as well as Oxford. Certainly that choir is becoming well-known and loved on this side of the world.

I am now in the throes of packing, but wanted to get this posted before I leave Tasmania. I never get over the feeling of "back to school after the holidays" when I return from leave. I dislike it just as much every time, although once I get back I am happy to be there. I shall post this as I go to the Airport tomorrow.

My prayers are with you; I hope that you will be restored to health and some degree of activity.

Yours affectionately,

---

245 Avalon is a city on the east coast of Australia. Biggs stopped in Avalon for a few days on her way home from leave.

## 82

13 May 1973

My dear Warren,

You have been a lot in my thoughts and I am surprised to find that I have no record of having written to you since my return from Australia. I was sure that I had written from New Guinea, but apparently my memory is at fault again. It is quite possible that you are not feeling well enough to write, and maybe it is too much to ask your Mr. Miller to write to <u>all</u> your correspondents to let them know how you fare. So I just wonder how you are and remember you in my prayers (when they are not too scrappy or occupied with local things!) and hope that you are not suffering. I wonder if you are still in your beloved Ireland? And if Mr. Miller goes across to see to your needs regularly?

Summer will be coming and that may well help to improve your condition. Do you read? Or have many visitors? I suppose modern Hospitals supply television and/or radio for the patients; that is fine so long as you can turn them off if you don't want them!

I have a new address, though the old one will still find me, as all Anglican mail in Popondetta goes through the Mission office and is sorted there. We move out of St. Luke's next month and already are stocktaking and listing things for removal elsewhere. I would like to be allowed to give some of our equipment to our Mission Hospitals, but fear that the Public Health Department will not agree to too much.

Irene Markham and I are living together in quite a nice little house in Popondetta town. It is very pleasant in many ways, but very noisy. The house is on the one main road and after payday the noise at night is pretty awful. Many of our Papuan brethren spend a large part of their pay on drink. However, it is pleasant to live where everyone knows one; I am always being greeted by name by Papuans and I don't know who they are. They are probably old patients or relatives of old patients. I work a lot in the Popondetta Hospital as a base, but am doing a lot of traveling too. Irene and I spend (usually) two days a week at St. Luke's. Apart from the typist in the office and the doctor in charge of the Hospital, I am the only expatriate in the medical set-up here. It is interesting to work with the indigenous people and see how they tackle work formerly done by whites; they are much more indirect and leisurely in their approach to problems but they get most of the essentials done with not too much strain on their blood pressure! There are only six more months until self-government is established. The trading and plantation people are worried about the future, but Missions seem to think that they can hand over gracefully and at a sensible pace. As most of the members of Parliament have been educated by some

Mission body or other, the Missions are in pretty high favour with the Government. I expect to retire at the end of the year, and hope that PHD (Public Health Department) will find someone to take my place before the end of the year so that I can hand over a pretty complicated job at leisure.

The Church here is pretty strong; we were the first here of course but as the Town has grown, other denominations have established themselves—United Church, Roman Catholics, Lutherans (and between all these relationships are very friendly) and Seventh Day Adventists and Jehovah's Witnesses.

Irene and I walked out to the Friary for Church this morning, an hour's walk through the bush before the sun had any heat. It was delightful, though a river we had to wade across had a current that took some strength to stand against—and lots of pebbles which we had to empty out of our sandals! The road is so rough that I avoid taking the motorbike out until the grader has been on it to smooth it out. The Friars had a Profession of a new Brother, simple but very impressive. The Friars are experimenting in hymns, both words and music, and are evolving a very real and appropriate method of worship. Much better than local translations of English hymns to English tunes! The Gloria and Sanctus and so on are quite thrilling, accompanied by a guitar or two, and drums and homemade percussion of odd variety. And plenty of young men to sing. We use simplified but meaningful English—e.g. Holy Ghost is replaced by Holy Spirit; and "quick" becomes "living".

Wishing you all good things, especially freedom from

pain; and the ability to enjoy any good things of life that come your way,

Yours affectionately,

# 83

2 May 1973

*[Note: This letter is handwritten rather than typed.]*

Dear Miss Biggs,

This is to tell you that the Major passed suddenly away on the 9th April. He is buried with his brother in the village churchyard. We managed to get him home from Ireland at the beginning of April. He seemed to be holding his own. The doctor checked him up and it was decided he needed a new pacemaker. Whilst the doctor was writing out a note to be taken in the ambulance with him, he seemed to decide he couldn't take any more and just quietly went to sleep and that was the end.

Yours sincerely,
L. Miller

# 84

27 May 1973

Dear Mr. Miller,

I am very grateful to you for letting me know of the Major's death. Your letter to me must have crossed one I had written to him. It might as well be destroyed now. It was not a surprise to me, since he had been in Hospital for so long; and in a way I was prepared for the news; but I shall miss his letters and his interest. I think he would be happy to go and be with his brother again in Paradise.

I am planning to visit England, maybe in a year's time; and always hoped that I could visit Major Lewis and meet him after all these years; now I can only plan to visit his grave and that of his brother. It is good to know that Kiln Lane has been given a new name to remember them.

You and your wife will be wondering now about your own future. Are you likely to stay on in the house as caretakers? I believe a good many tourists visit it each year.

With many thanks,
Yours sincerely,

*Note: In the springtime of 1974, Blanche Biggs finally made her trip to England and to Oxford, where she visited Warren Lewis's home, and his church, and his grave.*

# 85

24 June 1975

Dear Mr. Miller,

It is just a year since I was in Oxford, and you showed me both Oxford and the Lewis home. I have been reading my diary again, and remembering how much I valued that visit and enjoyed your kindness in showing me round. And so I thought I would write and tell you so.

I wonder how you are, and especially how Mrs. Miller has been keeping? I am afraid that the winter months must make it hard for people as they get older.

A few months ago in Tasmania, they asked me to speak at a Church service in one of the Hobart parishes. The Rector and his wife asked us in for a cup of tea after the service, and I found that he had done his training in one of the smaller Theological Colleges in Oxford, rather late in life, while he and his family had lived in Eynsham![246] So that was another

---

246 When Warren Lewis died, his will provided the Millers with enough money to purchase a home in Eynsham, a small village about 5 miles (8 km) north-east of Oxford.

link.

I bought the Biography of your "Master Jack" written by Roger Green and enjoyed it very much.[247] I also have the book with all the photographs in it, with good ones of you and Mrs. Miller, and lots of the house and the surroundings in Headington.[248] The house was being repaired when you took me there, as I suppose you remember; but by now it should be in good order and a joy to live in. My photographs of the house, and of the grave, and of the Church with you standing near the door, all came out very well. I find it very hard to picture just where the rooms were in that house: I don't suppose you could draw a plan of it for me, from memory? I myself drew a rough one, but there are blanks in the plan I can't fill in.

I have settled down in Brisbane, which is much warmer than Tasmania, and even now in the middle of winter, the sun is warm in the middle of the day. I have been doing a refresher course in medical work, and hope to do a bit of medical work; perhaps among the Aboriginals who are pretty plentiful in this city, and need medical care. Also I am living in a hostel and being a sort of Matron to 50 students, university and other Colleges; this is for a short time and then I plan to live in a small unit of my own, rather like the one you live in. Then in addition to medical work, I might do a bit of

247 Biggs is referring to *C. S. Lewis: A Biography* by Roger Lancelyn Green and Walter Hooper, published in 1974.

248 "The book with all the photographs in it" is probably *C. S. Lewis: Images of His World* by Douglas Gilbert and Clyde S. Kilby, published in 1973.

writing. The Major encouraged me in that hope of mine, and I hope it will be possible.[249]

With all good wishes to you both,

Yours very sincerely,

---

249 Blanche Biggs did write a book, entitled *From Papua with Love*. It was published in 1987.

# 86

12 July 1975

Dear Miss Biggs,

We were very pleased to get a letter from you. As you say it was a year since you were here and what a pleasant visit it was. Molly's general health seems a little better but her eyes and memory seem worse but then we are both over 74 so we can't expect too much. We haven't been down to see The Kilns since we went with you, but I believe they have made lots of changes. Enclosed you will find a very rough drawing of the house and I hope you will be able to follow them. We are having a very good summer. The best we have had for some years. Very pleased to hear that you are keeping busy and hope you will make a success of writing. Hoping to hear from you again soon.

Yours sincerely,
Len Miller

## 87

21 June 1978

Dear Miss Biggs,

I was very pleased to get a letter from you. I hope I have a chance to see you before you return to Australia. My news is not good. I lost my wife a year ago last Oct. Am rather lost on my own. When you rang me I must have been away. I have been to Switzerland for a holiday. If you are in Oxford again let me know and I will try to see you. As you know Molly was an invalid and I didn't get to meet many people. Here I am just getting to know a few more now but I am not enjoying living on my own. Thank you again for your letter. Am hoping to see you.

    Yours sincerely,

    Len

*The letters end here.*

## Afterword
*Meredith Goehring*

In Warren Lewis's final letter to Blanche Biggs, he concludes: "Yes, I hope I live to meet you, but in the meantime all blessings attend you. As ever, Warren." He died ten months later, an abrupt and unexpected end. When Blanche's long-awaited retirement finally arrived, she traveled to Oxford to visit The Kilns, as well as Warren's church and grave. It was no small feat for Blanche to complete the journey; it was a difficult trip physically as well as financially. It is a tribute to the extent of her regard for Warren that she made the trip at all, erasing the miles between them in a pilgrimage both of them had hoped would have a different ending.

## Blanche Biggs

After her trip, Blanche moved into a retirement community in Brisbane, where she spent the next 34 years. The transition was bittersweet. In a newsletter sent on February 6, 1974, Blanche writes,

> New Guinea has said goodbye to me, and I to New Guinea. The last weeks were so busy and demanding that I scarcely realized the implications of all the handing over: nor do I yet. It is a bit like having a tooth out under anesthesia, and the pain comes on as the anesthesia wears off! (Newsletter 110)

She lived independently there, spending time with friends and good books. John Biggs observes: "The art of living simply and lovingly she brought back with her to Brisbane." He adds, "What impressed and delighted me about her, even if it was at times uncomfortable, was that she could cut right through to the moral centre of any issue under discussion."[250] This simplicity, clarity, and directness are clear and present in these letters to Warren Lewis.

Blanche's commitment to Christ steered her life. Just as it guided her through her years of service in Papua, her faith guided her during her last years. Even in retirement, when she had settled in Brisbane, she sought opportunities to serve: "I have been doing a refresher course in medical work, and hope to do a bit of medical work; perhaps among the aboriginals who are pretty plentiful in this city, and need medical care" (Letter 85). She emphasized an open attitude to people no

---

250 The quotations from John Biggs included in this afterword are taken from the (unpublished) text of Blanche Biggs' obituary, delivered at her funeral on May 12, 2008.

matter their abilities or background, writing that the hospital tried to create a spirit "of service and friendship to all, regardless of barriers" (Newsletter 8). She carried this conviction to the end of her life, remaining a robust and servant-hearted woman all her days.

As she approached her 90th birthday, her good health faded. She suffered multiple health crises in her last decade, "each of which," as her nephew says, "she hoped would deliver her to her Maker, who she yearned to meet face to face." Blanche herself says little about this yearning, but her nephew John Biggs believes that her point of view was much the same as that of her grandmother Harriet Burville:

> It may be that I am nearly home... but I am not a bit afraid. My precious Jesus, who has never left nor forsaken me in all the years since I gave myself to Him, has taken away all fear of death... my whole trust is in the finished work of my Saviour, who is always my constant, ever-present Friend, close enough to be touched [...] I have not gone home yet, but waiting, trusting, and longing to go, and yet quite willing to stay here as long as my loving Father pleases. ... His will be done.

Blanche Biggs died on May 7, 2008. Her ashes are scattered in the rose garden of the Kenmore Parish Church (Queensland), where she was an active member. The papers, letters, and photographs that she had collected over the years were not destroyed: she donated her correspondence with Warren Lewis to The Marion E. Wade Center in Wheaton,

Illinois, and the rest of her accumulated papers, diaries, and photographs to the special collection at the Fryer Library, the University of Queensland.

## Early Years

Blanche Biggs did not always intend to devote a lifetime to the mission field. Born on the 20th of December, 1909, in North East Tasmania, she was the youngest child in a family of ten. In her last years at secondary school, she decided that she wanted to study medicine. From pocket money and various odd jobs, she saved one shilling a week until she had enough to enter nursing school.

While a student, she contracted tuberculosis. In those days, tuberculosis was often a death sentence. She spent six months in a sanatorium and following that, six years being cared for by her parents. During those years, she grew very close to her mother. They both prayed, and they believed that God heard their prayers. After long years of convalescence, Blanche was pronounced completely cured, and she went on to finish her medical degree at Melbourne University.

Soon after, while attending an Anglican church service at St. Peter's Eastern Hill in Melbourne, she heard a visiting preacher appeal for medical missionaries willing to go to Papua New Guinea. Blanche believed that God was telling her why He had answered her prayers for healing. Blanche took several extra courses in tropical medicine and received training as a midwife. Then, on the 7th of September, 1948, she was appointed by the Australian Board of Missions to the mission field.

Blanche spent the next 25 years serving in Papua New Guinea. She specialized in tuberculosis cases and worked among those with leprosy. But, as is often the case in mission hospitals, Blanche was also called upon to provide whatever medical care might be needed: delivering babies, tending to burns, and performing surgeries. In one of her early newsletters from the mission field, she describes an encounter with one patient as follows:

> Since I wrote last, I have done a fair amount of traveling, finally collected all my straggling bits of luggage and unpacked; and can fairly say that I have settled in. There have been odds and ends of surgery, none of it major; the most alarming thing I have done so far has been to repair a man's arm after a crocodile had finished with it. Both the patient and I, I think, offered up thanks that it was a small crocodile. In spite of the filth that crocodiles are credited with carrying in their teeth, the wound healed by first intention. (Newsletter 2)

This crocodile encounter occurred during her first year of service in Papua; her tone expresses a robust sense of adventure and curiosity that would sustain her through the next 24 years. She continues, "There are plenty of most interesting medical problems here, and one often longs for up-to-date laboratory facilities; however, one must go 'by guess and by

God' and leave it at that" (Newsletter 2). Though she was often overwhelmed by the amount of work she faced, she seemed undaunted by the challenges of the jungle.

Blanche did it all; she hosted Bishops and managed Church conferences and inoculated children against polio. Throughout her time on the mission field, she held two full-time jobs: as a hospital administrator and as a doctor who served as a midwife, primary care physician, and surgeon. In 1950, a year and a half into her tenure in Papua, she was presented with a little girl whose lips had been fused together by a tropical infection. Known colloquially as "yaws," this infection causes areas of the skin to swell and burst, forming lesions. Blanche writes that the girl was kept home from school and could only whisper. Blanche restructured the girl's lips in surgery and was "rewarded by a funny little smile" the first day she dressed the girl's wounds (Newsletter 10).

Tuberculosis was (and still is) one of the most prominent killers in Papua New Guinea; it was one of Blanche's fiercest challenges. She and her fellow missionaries were able to cure most of the cases brought to them. For example, she treated one woman with hardly any lung function. She had wasted to a mere skeleton. However, after receiving care in the hospital, the woman's appetite returned, and she was strong enough to participate in the mission's Christmas festivities (Newsletter 65). Blanche cared for everyone she could.

During her time in Papua, Blanche was awarded the Order of the British Empire. John Biggs notes, "Her OBE was the only instance where she might have been accused of the sin of pride." In trying to sum up his aunt's life and contributions, he writes, "She firmly believed that God had guided her life, and that intercession by prayer worked." He concludes, "Her oldest sister, Lil, was a saintly saint, her other sister, Win, a worldly saint [...], Blanche, the youngest of the three surviving sisters, was a feisty saint; a saint who pulled no punches."

## Even After

In October of 1968, Blanche wrote the very first of these letters to Warren. In it, she ponders the merits of burning her extensive memorabilia of documents, photographs, and journals, collected over a lifetime. Then she hesitates: "Some of my letters and papers might be useful in the future, even after my death, not because of their merit in themselves; but I have been a missionary doctor living in this same area for 20 years, and I have seen this Territory developing right under my nose, from primitive life to a pseudo-civilized one" (Letter 1). Blanche was wise to consider that her letters and papers might be useful one day. They offer a genuine portrait of life as a missionary in Papua New Guinea in the mid-1900s, articulated with candid authenticity.

Blanche wrote for the joy of self-expression and connection with her reader. It is a gift to us, the audience Blanche would never have imagined, that one of those favored readers was Warren Lewis. It was certainly a treasure to him. Warren's connection with a missionary doctor across the seas enriches our understanding not just of the elusive Major, but also of the Lewis brothers and the Inklings.

Blanche and Warren's story entrusts us with the same charge as the greatest tales: to live sacrificially for the sake of the good we see, both in the world and in one another. Blanche's story in particular is engaging and inspiring in its own right, and more: it is a reminder of generations of unsung heroes—missionaries and others—whose own stories deserve to be told.

# BIBLIOGRAPHY

*The Alternative Service Book*. London: SPCK, 1980.

Biggs, Blanche. *From Papua with Love*. Sydney: Australian Board of Missions, 1987.

Biggs, John. *Tasmania Over Five Generations: Return to Van Diemen's Land*. Tasmania: Forty Degrees South Publishing, 2011.

*Buk Baibel long Tok Pisin, or The Holy Bible with Deuterocanon in the Tok Pisin*. Albuquerque: Faith Comes by Hearing, 1969.

Courage, Michael, and Dermot Wright. *New Guinea Venture*. London: Robert Hale, Ltd., 1967.

Gilbert, Douglas, and Clyde S. Kilby. *C. S. Lewis: Images of His World*. Grand Rapids: Eerdmans, 1973.

Green, Roger Lancelyn, and Walter Hooper. *C. S. Lewis: A Biography*. New York: Harcourt Brace, 1974.

Gresham, Douglas H. *Lenten Lands: My Childhood with Joy Davidman and C. S. Lewis*. San Francisco: HarperOne, 2003.

Hadfield, Alice Mary. *An Introduction to Charles Williams.* London: Robert Hale, Ltd., 1959.

Heck, Joel D. "Warren Hamilton Lewis: His Brother's Brother." *The Chronicle of the Oxford University C. S. Lewis Society* 6, no. 3 (2009): 3-22.

Hooper, Walter. *C. S. Lewis: A Companion and Guide.* New York: Harper Collins Publishers, 1996.

Keller, Werner. *The Bible as History: Archaeology Confirms the Book of Books.* London: Hodder & Stoughton, 1956.

Kipling, Rudyard. "Recessional." *Poetry Foundation.* https://www.poetryfoundation.org/poems/46780/. Retrieved 10 April 2023.

Lewis, C. S. *The Allegory of Love: A Study in Medieval Tradition.* Oxford: Clarendon, 1936.

_____. "Answers to Questions on Christianity." In *God in the Dock*, edited by Walter Hooper, 61-62. Grand Rapids: Eerdmans, 1970.

_____. *The Collected Letters of C. S. Lewis, Volume I: Family Letters 1905-1931.* Edited by Walter Hooper. New York: HarperCollins Publishers, 2004.

_____. *The Collected Letters of C. S. Lewis, Volume II: Books, Broadcasts, and the War 1931-1949.* Edited by Walter Hooper. New York: HarperCollins Publishers, 2009.

_____. *The Four Loves: Featuring the Vintage BBC Recordings of C. S. Lewis.* Grand Haven, MI: Thomas Nelson on Brilliance Audio, 2017.

_____. *Letters to an American Lady.* Grand Rapids: Eerdmans, 2014.

_____. *Letters of C. S. Lewis.* Edited by W. H. Lewis and

Walter Hooper. San Francisco: HarperOne Publishing, 2017.

_____. *Letters to Malcolm: Chiefly on Prayer*. Boston: Harcourt, 1964.

Lewis, W. H. *Brothers and Friends: The Diaries of Major Warren Hamilton Lewis*. Edited by Clyde S. Kilby and Majorie Lamp Mead. San Francisco: Harper & Row, 1982.

_____, ed. *The Memoirs of the Duc de Saint-Simon*. London: Macmillan *1964*.

_____. *The Splendid Century. Life in the France of Louis XIV*. New York: William Sloane Assoc., 1953.

"Major W. H. Lewis: Soldier and Writer, Obituary." *The (London) Times*. April 16, 1973.

McCarthy, John Keith. *Patrol into Yesterday: My New Guinea Years*. Melbourne: F. W. Chesire, 1963.

Sayer, George. *Jack: A Life of C. S. Lewis*. Wheaton: Crossway Books, 1988.

Verney, Stephen. *Fire in Coventry: How Love, Prayer, and the Holy Spirit Completely Transformed a Congregation*. Westwood, NJ: Revell, 1964.

Williams, Charles. *The Place of the Lion*. London: Victor Gollancz, Ltd., 1931.

## READING WHAT THEY READ
### A List of Books Mentioned in
### the Letters of Warren Lewis and Blanche Biggs

Other authors mentioned include Mary Stewart, John Buchan, Dorothy L. Sayers, Clyde S. Kilby, Robert Browning, St. Francis of Assisi, Josephus, and Charlotte Mary Yonge.

Benson, James. *Prisoner's Base and Home Again: The Story of a Missionary P.O.W.*
Blamires, Harry. *Blessing Unbounded: A Vision.*
_____. *Devil's Hunting Ground.*
_____. *Cold War in Hell.*
_____. *Highway to Heaven.*
Bone, Edith. *Seven Years Solitary.*
*Book of Common Prayer.*
Bonhoeffer, Dietrich. *Letters and Papers from Prison.*
Caskie, Donald. *The Tartan Pimpernel.*
Davidman, Joy. *Smoke on the Mountain: An Interpretation of the Ten Commandments*
Gilbert, Douglas and Clyde S. Kilby. *C. S. Lewis: Images of*

*His World.*

Green, Roger Lancelyn and Walter Hooper. *C. S. Lewis: A Biography.*

Hadfield, Alice Mary. *An Introduction to Charles Williams.*

Hope, Anthony. *The Prisoner of Zenda.*

Keller, Werner. *The Bible as History: Archaeology Confirms the Book of Books.*

Lewis, C. S. *The Case for Christianity.*

_____. *Christian Behavior.*

_____. *Christian Reflections.*

_____. *The Four Loves.*

_____. *The Great Divorce.*

_____. *The Horse and His Boy.*

_____. *Letters of C. S. Lewis.*

_____. *Letters to an American Lady.*

_____. *Letters to Malcolm: Chiefly on Prayer.*

_____. *Miracles: A Preliminary Study.*

_____. *Reflections on the Psalms.*

_____. *The Screwtape Letters.*

Lewis, W. H. *The Sunset of the Splendid Century.*

Muggeridge, Malcolm. *Jesus Rediscovered.*

*The New English Bible.*

Phillips, J. B. *Ring of Truth: A Translator's Testimony.*

_____. *Your God is Too Small.*

Shakespeare, William. *A Midsummer Night's Dream.*

Strong, Philip. *The New Guinea Diaries of Philip Strong 1936-45.*

Tolkien, J. R. R. *The Lord of the Rings.*

Trollope, Anthony. *Australia and New Zealand.*

Woodforde, James. *Diary of a Country Parson, 1758-1802.*

## Acknowledgments

I am profoundly grateful for my many collaborators:

The C. S. Lewis and the Inklings Society, the C. S. Lewis Foundation, the Southern California C. S. Lewis Society, the Mythopoeic Society, Taylor University, and Azusa Pacific University, for sponsoring pre-publication presentations of this work;

David Esselstrom, Department Chair; Jennifer Walsh, Dean of the College of Liberal Arts and Sciences; David Weeks, Dean of the Honors College; and Mark Stanton, Provost, for approving my sabbatical and supporting this project;

Marjorie Lamp Mead, Laura Schmidt, and the rest of the staff at the wonderful Wade Center;

Michael Ward, for being the very first to embody these words from Major Lewis;

Scott and Mary Key, who believed in this project year after year. Your faith was the fuel that kept me going;

Barbara Hayes, Sarah O'Dell, Megan Brand, Rhonda Roberts, and so many others who took time to look over drafts, niggle over commas, and argue over spelling: I could not have endured the last miles of this marathon without you;

Pete Peterson and the visionary staff of The Rabbit Room: You made this a better book. You made a dream come true;

Ann Wilson, who typed and checked and rechecked all over again and did not let a single blunder pass her by;

Roger White, for encouragement, criticism, and welcome suggestions;

Don W. King, for answering obscure, pesky, persistent questions with characteristic speed and grace;

Linda Sherman Spitser: everything you touch, you improve;

David Bratman, one of my favorite collaborators;

Andrew Lazo, who never stopped believing that there were new chapters yet to be written;

Reggie and Teana Weems, for help tracking down the smallest details;

The sprawling, varied online Inklings community for checking facts and providing information, insight, and encouragement through the long years of this project;

Simon Farley, Belinda Spinaze, and the rest of the staff at the Fryer Library at The University of Queensland, for their energetic assistance with the Blanche Biggs papers and diaries;

John Biggs, for generously providing so much insight and information about his family;

Joel D. Heck, whose chronology was invaluable to this research;

Team Bandersnatch: Danielle Coleman, Josie Zimmerman, Meredith Goehring, Lucille Chavez, Sierra Glyer, and Brianna Askew for researching tiny details, tracking down obscure information, writing up footnotes, eating lots of chocolate, and sustaining me through yet another project;

And The Niños. Without prayer, there would be no books.

# INDEX

Donegal 93
Duke of Windsor 243
du Maine, duc 88, 95
Dutch Reformed Church 252

**E**

Easter Rising in Dublin (1916)
 134
electric strike, in England
 147–148, 152
Elliot, Nancy A. 90, 99, 127,
 205–206
 arrived in England 118–119
 back in Australia from overseas
  trip 125
 born giver 59
 and "charity" 58–59
 desire to Warren 95
 England visit, experience of 135
 gift of tour, accepting 64–65
 overseas trip of 86, 111
 resigned 205
 retirement of 198, 207
 wrote to priest of Franciscans
  58
"Empire Day" 94, 98
Empire Music Hall 220
England 236
 beef shortage in 241, 247
 Blanche's long-planned trip to
  238
 calling by title in 104
 coal strike in 221, 222–223
 cost of living in 112
 dock strike 233n228, 241
 electric strike in 147–148, 152
 hospitality in 107
 industrial troubles in 233

joining Common Market 199,
 202
 Queen's pocket money 206,
  207
 railway strike 233, 241
 Rolls Royce closure 184
 seasons and weather in 31, 84,
  89, 125, 240, 248
 strikes in 130, 143, 236
 Trade Union Council 130n153
 violence and disorder 241
 voluntary donations from 24
 wages in 130
 Walkathons in 227
 Warren offers book on 30
*entre nous* 201
Eroro Mission 196–197
Esquimo Bible 83
Eucharist 153
Eucharistic Congress 264

**F**

fibrositis 41
*Fire in Coventry* (Verney) 34n52
Flying Squads 116
France
 17th century 51
 Warren's interest in 17th
  century 55–56
Franciscans at Cambridge 43
frangipani 220, 225–226
Freud, June 5n14
Friars 43, 78, 268
 Cambridge 228
 Church worship, use of guitars
  in 121
 writing hymns 121

# RABBIT ROOM
## ~ PRESS ~

NASHVILLE, TENNESSEE

## The
# RABBIT ROOM

The Rabbit Room (named for the back room of the pub
where the Inklings —J. R. R. Tolkien, C. S. Lewis,
Charles Williams, and others—shared their stories)
cultivates and curates story, music, and art
to nourish Christ-centered communities
for the life of the world.

*For more information visit:*
**WWW.RABBITROOM.COM**

# But wait!
# There's more!

Want learn more about Diana Pavlac Glyer and her work? Use the QR code below or visit DianaGlyer.com.

Want to share the story of Blanche and Warren with others? *The Major & the Missionary* has also been adapted into a one-act play.

If you'd like to bring their story to a stage in your area, visit DianaGlyer.com for more information.